VOLU

INSPIRING MOTIVATIONAL POWERFUL ACRONYMS

for COGNITIVE THINKING

I • M • P • A • C • T

JEN DU PLESSIS

IMPACT

Inspiring Motivational Powerful Acronyms
for Cognitive Thinking

Jen Du Plessis

Joint Venture Publishing

Blue Sky R&D, LLC

Printed in the United States of America

Table of Contents

A.N.M.N.N.

A • No • Means • Not • Now

ALEC STERN

I learned quite early in life just how to turn a No into a Yes. I remember many hot summer days as a child asking my Mom for an ice cream. Usually the answer was No – it was going to spoil my appetite for dinner. I would do some chores then ask again. This time, her response would be different – she would thank me for helping her out then tell me I could have the ice cream.

Fast forward some years and, as I began my business career, I carried with me the important lesson I learned, "A No Means Not Now."

When talking to prospective customers, mentors, strategic partners, and investors, you will often receive a No regarding their interest or willingness to engage with you to hear more.

Here are a few tips on how to turn a No into a Yes. First, ask if this is a good time to speak or if they would prefer to schedule a later time. This will confirm they are ready to engage and receive the information you will be providing them.

When approaching a conversation, always lead with value and ask questions of the person you are speaking to. If you are talking to a prospective customer you could ask, "What are your goals and vision for your business?" "What do you have in business today that you wished you had more of?" "What don't you have in business today and wish you did?" "Are you looking to save time, save money, increase revenue, customers, etc.?"

From their responses you can tailor an interaction that will resonate with them and open the door for a follow-up conversation. Keep your comments short and to the point and address what they have shared. Do not "Spray and Pray." This is where you just keep talking (and talking) and pray they hear something that interests them.

When listening to others, it's pretty common to be thinking of what we are going to say when they are done speaking. Don't do this! Be present and listen to what the prospect is really saying. (If you take the letters of the word LISTEN and mix them up, you can spell SILENT!) Active listening helps you guide your responses to make them relevant to the prospect's vision, goals, etc. So, be an active listener.

When you receive a No, ask why your presentation or approach didn't resonate. It could have been because of how you presented the information. Perhaps they were not receiving your words as intended, making it easier for them to say No. Feedback is a gift, so hearing your prospect's comments is a learning experience. Ask to stay in touch and be sure to follow through.

It's been said that most people say No five times before they say Yes. I learned early on not to let a No discourage me – and neither should you! In my experience, some one-time No's have led to new customers, strategic partners, mentors, investors, referrals and more. It will take practice, it will require sharpening your active listening skills, and it will mean revising and rethinking your approach – likely more than once.

Over time you will cultivate the relationships you desire – just keep reminding yourself that "A No Means Not Now."

Learn more at: http://www.alecspeaks.com.

ALEC STERN

 Alec Stern has more than 25 years of experience as a founder, mentor, investor, and hyper-growth agent for companies across various industries. He is an innovator with extensive expertise in growing and scaling companies, startup and operational growth, go-to-market strategy, strategic partnerships and more.

As a primary member of Constant Contact's founding team, Alec was one of the original 3 who started the company in an attic. Alec was with the company for 18 years from start-up, to IPO, to a $1.1 Billion-dollar acquisition. Alec has also been a co-founder or on the founding team of several other successful startups, including VMark (IPO & acquisition), Reacher Grasper Cane and MOST Cardio, amongst others.

Performing hundreds of keynote addresses worldwide, Alec has become known as America's Startup Success Expert for his popular sessions at conferences like Secret Knock, CEO Space International, City Summit, Powerteam International, and Habitude Warrior. In 2019, Alec was the Keynote speaker at three out of the top five "Inc. Magazine Must Attend Conferences for Startups and Entrepreneurs in 2019." While on tour, Alec has shared the stage with the likes of Tom Bilyeu, Jack Canfield, Les Brown, Kevin Harrington, and Mark Victor Hanson. Alec appears on the Influence 100 Authority List by *Influence Magazine*, which recognizes his contribution to helping and advancing startups and entrepreneurs worldwide. He has also recently been featured on the covers of several other magazines, including *Small Business Trendsetters*, *Success Profiles*, and *Business Innovators*. Alec was honored with the "2020 City Gala Visionary Award" and the "Habitude Warrior Conference Global Awesome Visionary Award" for all his accomplishments as an entrepreneur, as well as speaking before thousands of entrepreneurs and startups each year.

Alec advises a variety of early-stage companies and serves as a judge, mentor, and advisor for nationally known startup accelerators and programs, including TechStars, MassChallenge, The American Business Awards, and The Stevie Awards, and speaks at universities, including Harvard and MIT.

Only a sideman when it comes to music, Alec is an accomplished drummer and has had the honor of sitting in with a number of musicians, including Toby Keith's house band in Vegas.

B.L.I.S.S.

Believe • Love • Integrate • Smile • Serve

MONEEKA SAWYER

A few years ago, I wrote my heart's message in a book and sent it out into the world. This book poured out of me with passion, love, and conviction to help the world. The book was called *Choose Bliss: The Power and Practice of Joy and Contentment.* I was delighted at the reception the book got from the public and had so much fun traveling the country and the world doing a TV tour, speaking on many amazing stages, and sharing my voice on radio and podcasts. The world obviously wanted more bliss, and I was so excited to share my ideas on how to make that happen.

As I travelled, spoke, and got to know my readers, I realized I needed a way to capture their minds so they could easily remember how to bring bliss into their lives day by day, and even minute by minute. That's when I created the BLISS acronym that I'm sharing with you now.

B is for BELIEVE!

In order for you to create anything in your life, you must believe it can be done. When I talk about bliss, I'm not talking about something that just happens in your life. It is not circumstantial or at the mercy of what is happening outside of you. Instead, it is a way of being. It is something you create inside of you. You cannot control what happens outside of you. But if you want a blissful life, you must control what happens inside. In order to do that you must BELIEVE that it is possible.

The next piece is to believe you can learn how to do it. You need to believe that living blissfully is a learnable skill. That you have control over it, and that it is your choice. If you believe you can learn it, you will then be willing to find the resources to help you to learn it.

And finally, you must move into believing that you can be, do, and have bliss. No matter what is going on for you in your life, you are in control of your bliss. This is where BELIEVE turns into magic. Your **belief** in your ability to choose, in your ability to create a blissful life and in yourself, is the first step to getting you there.

L is for LOVE

Bliss cannot happen without love. There are three aspects to love that will help you bring bliss into your life.

Love yourself. You were born with yourself, and you will leave this life with yourself. You are the only person you will be in a relationship with for your entire life. Doesn't it make sense that you should have a loving relationship with yourself? Most of us focus on the relationships outside of ourselves and forget that those relationships are only secondary to our longest-term relationship, the relationship with ourselves. Start paying attention to how you speak to yourself, what you expect of yourself, and how you feel about yourself. Are you kind, respectful, and loving? If not, you need to learn how to be. Learn how to love yourself first. You can't be truly blissful until you truly love yourself.

Love your life. The master skill of bliss is gratitude. And the way to feel an abundance of gratitude is to truly love your life. To constantly search for, focus on, and be grateful for all those things you love in your life. The more you look for what you love in your life, the more you will find. And you will get better and better at this the more you practice.

Love people without judgement. While our families are an exception, for the most part we can choose the people we work with, play with, and build our lives with. With all of these people, even our families, we can choose whether we are going to have a relationship with them and spend time with them. If we decide to have relationships with these people, why not choose to do it blissfully? This doesn't mean the relationships will always be happy, it just means that you are taking a blissful approach to them, and therefore will feel blissful with them more of the time.

The first key to choosing bliss in relationships is to choose not to judge people. Judgment makes us feel bad and doesn't change anyone else's mind. Allow yourself to accept people as they are and understand that the only person you can change is you. If you are having an issue in a relationship, look at what you can alter in yourself to make the relationship work. I am not condoning abuse of any kind. However, most problems in relationships have nothing to do with abuse and more to do with a difference in opinions, beliefs, or expectations. These are things you can manage within yourself.

I is for INTEGRATE

I am a business coach specializing in helping people build passive wealth the blissful way. Because I'm in the coaching industry, I hear all the ways people are shamed for who they are. We are told our bodies need to look, feel, or perform a certain way. Or we're told to not focus on our bodies because that's too superficial. We're told that having guts is more important than being smart, and smart people are even maligned as not having any idea how to be successful. We're told that emotions are bad and make us weak. We're told that our ego is our ultimate enemy and must be silenced. We're told that spirituality is only for "New Agers." The list of shaming verbiage and beliefs goes on and on.

You can't be blissful if you are shaming yourself. Integration and acceptance of all of these parts of you is imperative to feeling bliss. All these parts of us were given to us for a reason. They each support us in having successful, blissful lives, and none of them work at their best without the support of the others. So, learn to accept all the amazing parts of you and integrate them all into how you live your life.

Keep your body healthy and fit so that it moves you physically through your life blissfully. Spend time learning each day so you can expand and grow your mind. Accept and honor your emotions. They give you signals about what is working in your life and what isn't. If you are having an emotional reaction to something, or feeling something very strongly, pay attention and learn lessons from those emotions. Then allow yourself to go back to the emotional equilibrium of bliss, taking the lessons with you. Understand that your ego is the part of you that moves you through your life. It is what motivates you to take action. Don't let it dominate who you are and what you do, but understand it's a part of you and a tool you can use and engage to create bliss in your life. And finally, spirituality (not necessarily organized religion) has been a focus of human beings since the beginning of time. Connecting to your spiritual side gives you access to your intuition, your inner knowing, your peace, and the true core of who you are.

In order to be blissful, integrate all these parts of yourself into your life. Accepting all of you, is a very important part of being blissful.

S is for SMILE

I know how simple this sounds, but in order to be blissful you must smile! There is clinical proof that people who smile have much more blissful lives.

Your body releases three hormones that make you feel good when you smile. These include endorphins, dopamine, and serotonin. These send signals to your body that you're happy, and in turn, you actually feel happier.

Author of *Smile: The Astonishing Powers of a Simple Act,* Ron Gutman said, "British researchers found that one smile can generate the same level of brain stimulation as up to 2,000 bars of chocolate." (And it doesn't have as many calories!) Even a pretend smile is better than no smile. While this doesn't feel natural, you can in fact make yourself feel better by simply forcing a smile.

So smile frequently and laugh often. Even when you don't feel like it... in fact *because* you don't feel like it. It will turn your feelings around and make you more blissful.

S is for SERVICE

A 2017 study done in collaboration with three universities around the world found that being of service to others benefits the giver by increasing their joy and contentment … their bliss. The study, using MRI's to study the neurological changes in the brain when someone is giving to others, found that the parts of the brain associated with joy light up when they give, monetarily or with deeds. This creates a heightened sense of bliss for the giver. This phenomenon has become known as the "Givers High." To increase the bliss in your life, start living your life with an attitude of service. Be kind, do kind deeds, contribute time and money to causes you believe in. Understand that giving to others can show up in many non-monetary forms. Give someone a smile, open a door, volunteer your time. The options are endless. And by adding "being of service" into your life, you will greatly increase the bliss of those around you as well as for yourself.

What is it that you want for your life? If you travel the path from what you *think* you want, and dig deeper to your core desire, you will find that everything you do is simply to increase your own happiness. This is true for everyone. So why not make that your primary goal above all else? Not just to be happy, but to be blissful. To feel joy and contentment with your life at all times. It really is in your power. It is your choice. Bliss is your birthright. Every single day you can always *Choose BLISS!*

Connect with Moneeka Sawyer and get your free gift at
Blissfulinvestor.com.

MONEEKA SAWYER

Moneeka Sawyer is the blissful millionaire. She has been investing in real estate for over 20 years, so has experienced all the different cycles of the market. Still, she has turned $10,000 into over $2,000,000, working only 5-10 hours per MONTH with very little stress.

Moneeka has helped countless people pay for their children's college educations and weddings, retire with the lifestyle they dreamed of, or just become millionaires. And they've all done this Moneeka's blissful way.

Moneeka is the best-selling author of *Choose Bliss: The Power and Practice of Joy and Contentment*. She is also the recipient of the Woman of Impact Quill award from *Focus on Women* magazine, and the Quill Award for Best Literary Work from the Governor of the State of Maryland. She hosts the podcast Real Estate Investing for Women and her expertise, and bliss-filled laugh, have been featured on stages, radio, podcasts, and TV stations, including ABC, CBS, and FOX, reaching over 150 million people.

Connect with Moneeka at Blissfulinvestor.com

B.Y.O.B.

Become • Your • Own • Bank

CHRIS NAUGLE

Society has taught us to spend, save, and live our lives in a way that is hurting us more than it's helping us. We give up our hard-earned dollars in exchange for products or services, never realizing the true cost of those traditional exchanges. A great example of this is how we buy our cars.

People typically buy cars in one of several ways, all of which involve borrowing money from an outside institution or giving up the opportunity to have our money work harder for us. We blindly dump our dollars into a depreciating asset and chalk it up to societal norms because that's what we've been taught, with no alternatives. My story starts out just the same as yours, with the same ill-founded knowledge.

As a young adult, I never questioned how much the bank or car company would be making off me as I exchanged monthly payments for the right to buy and drive my cars. For years, when it came to buying cars, I was doing it all wrong. I bought into what the car dealership was selling me about the value in leasing or financing.

I was not buying my cars like the wealthy would. The wealthy would never question how they could get money from the bank to buy a car; instead, they would ask how they could become the bank and make money off of their car purchases.

Building real wealth becomes possible only when you reclaim control of your finances and become your own bank (BYOB). And the process starts with analyzing two things: *how we think about money* and *how we approach our spending* (and saving).

There are three traditional ways to buy a car:

1. You pay cash for it.
2. You bank finance it.
3. You lease it.

Here's the real truth about these traditional methods to buying a car:

1. **Paying cash:** You can take money out of your bank and exchange it for a car that immediately depreciates as you drive it off the lot. By paying cash, you are losing the interest earning potential of the money you gave away to get the car.

2. **Bank financing:** By taking a loan from the bank or a finance company, you exchange monthly payments on the loan for the right to drive a car. Over a period of time, the loan to the bank is paid off and you rightfully own the car… just in time for the car to begin requiring more costly maintenance.

3. **Leasing a car:** In a lease, you are essentially renting your car. You exchange monthly payments for the right to drive a car, while staying within the strict mileage limits. After the lease, you return the car and walk away with nothing.

Each of these methods means you either:

1. Pay interest to another party, or
2. Give up interest you could have earned.

This second, silent financial killer is called "opportunity cost." It means that even for those of you who pay cash for your cars, all you are doing is making one large payment up front, versus making monthly payments over several years. Paying cash for your car also ***does not keep you from having to pay*** *interest.* For example, let's say you pay $25,000 cash for a car. That amount goes to the car company or bank. You've now given up the potential to earn interest on that $25,000 somewhere else.

But what if I told you that there is a *fourth option* that gives you the power to recapture some, most, or even all of the money you'll pay for all of the cars you will ever buy, drive and own? And that's on top of anything you get from selling those cars after you've enjoyed them for a few years! This fourth option is accomplished through the power of The Money Multiplier Method and the Infinite Banking Concept®, and it is based off of the three principles below:

1. *Pay Yourself First*
2. *Pay Yourself Back with Interest*
3. *Recycle and Recapture the Money You Spend*

The latter is precisely what you're doing when you get back every dollar you've spent on every car you'll ever buy, drive and own. Our team *specially designs* whole life insurance policies with mutually owned companies that pay dividends. This becomes your banking system.

This method really comes down to not relying on the bank for your financing needs, but rather, learning how the bank operates and using that knowledge to become your own bank! When you use your banking policy to buy a car you are simply recreating what the banks do: you're keeping your money moving.

For example, let's say you want to buy a car for $25,000. Let's assume that this is precisely the amount you have in your bank account—one that is paying you 4% interest. This is a much higher rate than any conventional bank would pay you, but for *your bank*, these are accurate numbers. You ask to take $25,000 of your money from the bank to pay cash for your car, but instead, your banker uses your account as collateral and gives you a loan at 6% interest on the $25,000. You agree and the funds are transferred to you.

Based on how banks work, the bank will end up making more on the 6% interest you'll pay them on your loan than you will on your 4% interest-bearing bank account. But what if I told you that your banker actually did you a favor by wanting to charge you 6% interest on the loan and leaving your money in your account, rather than having you take out the $25,000 in cash from your 4% interest-bearing account?

It's true. Let's look at the math:

- Your loan costs you $28,999 over sixty months ($25,000 loan + the 6% interest).

- In the meantime, the $25,000 you had in the 4% bank account has grown to $30,525 over the same sixty-month period.

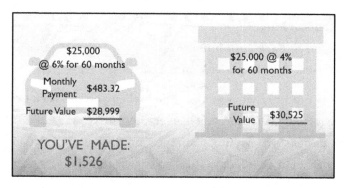

The reason you were better off taking the $25,000 loan at 6% and leaving your money in the bank is because the interest charged on the money the bank loaned you is simple interest, paid on a decreasing balance. Since you are paying back the $25,000 loan over time, the balance upon which interest is charged is always decreasing, and the 4% you're earning inside your bank account is always increasing, earning compound interest. Both of these things work to increase the balance on your account.

Our minds are programmed to think that if we borrow at 6% and earn at 4%, we're losing 2%, but that's not how money (or math) works. You can make money all day long by paying 6% and earning 4% by becoming your own bank and implementing The Money Multiplier Method.

So how can the average person take advantage of this system to earn all the money back for every car they will ever buy, drive, or own like the wealthy do?

1. **Do your homework.** Before we get to the part where you actually buy

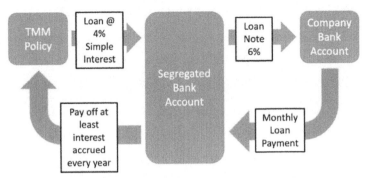

the car, make sure you determine the car you want, how much it's going to cost you in cash, and how much it would cost you if you decided to finance the car. You'll need both of these numbers.

2. **Prepare the funds.** Take a policy loan from your policy for the full purchase price of the car in cash.

3. **Buy the car.** After receiving the funds, deposit them into your bank account. Then, head to the car dealership and buy the car you want using the funds in your bank account.

4. **Be an honest banker.** Even though you purchased the car in cash, don't forget you used your banking policy to do so. And to be an honest banker and get the most out of your banking policy, you need to treat your money just the same as you'd treat the bank's money. This is where you'll use the number you got earlier in the process when you determined the amount you'd have to pay monthly if you financed the car, including interest! Write a check to your banking policy every month at that same amount for as long as the term would've been had you financed the car.

5. **Sell the car and begin again.** After your last payment is paid, you now have two options.

    a. You can sell your car right away, pocket the profit, and use your policy to begin the process over with a new car.

b. You can keep the car longer, sell (or not sell) whenever you wish, and start the process again with your next car.

Either way, you've now earned most (if not all) of the money back that you've used to purchase the car in the first place, *and* you've put additional funds into your pocket after you decided to sell your car.

As you can see, the process is quite simple. It can be easily duplicated over and over again to last your whole lifetime. And all you're doing is changing where your money goes first.

This process allows you to continue your normal spending habits (like buying cars), while building your wealth and living the life you want to live. We teach people just like you every day how to recycle and recapture all the money you are paying to everyone else, create real wealth, keep your money in your family, and leave the legacy you've always wanted t. It all happens when you make the decision to become the bank, set up your banking system, and take the loans that are available to you.

I can wholeheartedly say that the Infinite Banking Concept® helped me climb out of debt and fully redeem everything that happened during the hard times in my life. It was what empowered me to drive and own my dream car. And best of all, it was all done without my having to work any harder, without having to give away control of my money, and without taking on any additional risk. The same can be true for you. All you need to do is change one thing: *where your money goes first*!

Learn more at: moneyschoolrei.com/masterclass-replay-chris

CHRIS NAUGLE

 From pro-snowboarder to money mogul, Chris Naugle has dedicated his life to being America's #1 Money Mentor. His success includes managing over 30 million dollars in assets in the financial services and advisory industry and tens of millions in real estate business, with over 200 transactions and an HGTV pilot show since 2014.

Learn more at moneyschoolrei.com/masterclass-replay-chris

C.C.T.A.

Confidence • Competence • Trust • Approachability
KERSTIN O'SHIELDS

Our body is our communication tool. Being aware of how you engage others in conversation is essential because over 90% of our communication is nonverbal.

Human-to-human communication is broken down in this way: 55% is body movement, carriage, and facial expressions and 38% is vocal tone and vocal inflection. This leaves only 7% of our communication as the actual words we choose when we talk to each other.

Here is another way to look at it. The words are like the foundation of a house. We need words to give foundational structure to the message. But we can't live only on the foundation of a house alone. We need the framing, drywall, doors, and windows to give shape and function to the house. That is what body gestures and facial expressions do in a conversation. It carries the intention and meaning of the message.

The vocal tone is the curb appeal. The color on the walls and landscaping in the yard is what pulls on the heartstrings and makes it feel like home. Our vocal tone paints the emotions of what is said in our conversations to drive the message home to the heart.

If you are not intentional with your nonverbal communication to express what you are saying, you are missing out on the biggest part of human connection. And even worse, you could be expressing something completely different than you intended.

Just talking is not enough … You need to engage!

But how can you learn to engage your body language at a higher level? You focus on the Body Language Strategy Success Pillars: Confidence, Competence, Trust, and Approachability (CCTA).

With the CCTA Body Language Strategy Success Pillars, you magnetize a connection with others using this powerful approach to nonverbal communication. These pillars connect to our deep instincts as pack animals and determine how we distinguish who we are within our "tribes" or society. When you present yourself with the CCTA Success Pillars effectively, you are automatically looked at as a leader in your industry, knowledgeable in your field, easy to work with, and someone that people will happily want to connect with all without saying a word.

It is important to understand the function of each of these pillars:

Confidence: Your posture, breath, and energy levels are an unspoken social cue of your social and leadership status. Your body placement rules how your posture and your breath work together helping you to exude being present in every situation.

Competence: Fluidity in your body movement, speech patterns, and vocal projection physically express your level of knowledge and ability to engage others with grace and poise.

Trust: Creating an inviting presence that communicates being willing to work with others encourages trust with open body gestures and movement that demonstrate a balance of vulnerability and stability.

Approachability: Expressing your approachability by drawing in your audience with purposeful facial expressions that match your messaging creates an inviting presence and a stronger emotional bond.

Let's dig deeper into how each of the CCTA Success Pillars works.

Confidence

Body language starts from the inside out. As humans, we emotionally respond to what we physically see and hear. The core nonverbal attraction for humans is confidence, making it the cornerstone of all the pillars.

Good posture communicates confidence and authority. This is derived from the skeletal structure of the body supporting the function of your breath to energize every part of our nonverbal communication shown in the muscular carriage of the body. It also enhances your focus because your posture directly affects your ability to oxygenate your body. A well-oxygenated body and brain have a higher level of mental clarity and stamina helping you to bring your "A-Game" to every interaction.

This is the key starting point for showing up authentic and present. Being seen as competent, trustworthy, and kind is a good idea. However, doing all those things in a lackadaisical way instead of with confidence makes these efforts feel lukewarm or insincere.

That is why your posture is your number one presence tool. It enhances everything else you do!

Competence

Fluidity is the key to showing your competence in your body language. It is showcased through the grace of body movement and articulate vocal abilities in speech patterns, speech rate, and vocal tone.

Showing fluidity in your body gestures automatically makes you appear as if you are affluent and have a more elite presence no matter the activity. Because the mind is hardwired to the body, we intrinsically make the correlation that if you are showing a high-level physical capability, you mentally approach life the same way also.

Finding your balance in your body while you move will help the rest of your body move with ease, enhancing the competence perception. Learning to move with fluid motions and with grace can make the difference between having the appearance of being a high-end businessperson versus a novice, whether you have experience or not.

Fluidity is represented in our vocal abilities too. How we produce our words has a dramatically higher impact on how people perceive, and more importantly, respond to what you are saying. If you are fumbling over your words trying to explain an idea, you will be perceived as being less knowledgeable or not as good as others on the subject.

Vocal articulation, speech rate, and tone is an area that is often overlooked in presence training. This is unfortunate because it can have the biggest communication impact on whether you get the job at an interview or advance in your career.

Trust

In any situation, it is important to create trust. Business, family, and personal relationships all depend on trust to thrive. Trust is shown through body language with a positive, open position in the carriage of your torso to communicate you are willing to open your thoughts and emotions to those around you.

From underneath the jawbone down to the pelvic bone, we have an exceedingly small amount of the hardcover to protect the most vital organs in our bodies. In front of the body, we have some bone coverage called the ribs, but that is it... Everything else is exposed and only protected by skin and muscle that can be punctured. If you get stuck with something in your leg, it's going to hurt, however, it's not immediately life-threatening. If you get stuck anywhere in the torso, it could be potentially fatal.

Therefore, showing and opening this vulnerable part of our body to those in front of us is one of the unspoken social cues that show and invite trust. Putting the shoulders back and opening your arms so that the front of your body is exposed to another person or group is saying in a nonverbal way, "I am choosing to make my body vulnerable to you." Doing this with a balanced stature creates the feeling of stability, enhancing the perception that the person is fully committed to creating trust.

Because what we see physically is automatically transferred to what we perceive about others mentally, we start to see that person as not only showing trust, but also trustworthy.

Approachability

The eyes are the window of the soul. This age-old truth is anchored in the fact that we feel connected when we look at each other's eyes during a conversation or interaction.

Though we are looking at each other's eyes, what we are *responding* to is the movement of the muscles around the eyes. This is what tells the story of the emotions we are feeling making the top expression spot on the face the movement around your eyes and the eyebrows. This is referred to as "The Mask."

The Mask includes all muscle movement above the eyebrows, around the entire eye area, and down to the cheekbones. This is the same area of the face that would be covered if you were wearing a masquerade ball mask.

With a slight lift of the eyebrows, the entire eye area lifts and opens showing an unspoken social cue of interest. That makes us feel good when we are talking to someone and see that they are engaged in what we are sharing. When we see someone is showing interest on their face, we tend to naturally open up and are more drawn into the conversation.

It is also not just about engaging the Mask while you are talking. You also must engage it while you are listening. Keeping that engagement on both sides of the conversation (talking and listening), makes you come across as a person who genuinely cares and is easy to talk to about anything.

Let's put this all together: think of a person you just love talking to. Usually, you enjoy interacting with this person because they are looking at you while you talk, sitting open and relaxed in their body gestures, smiling, and responding with a relaxed tone. This makes you feel seen and heard in your conversations with them. This engagement encourages you to want to know more about this person and makes it easier to create a deeper connection without even trying.

The result of layering the CCTA Body Language Success Pillars effectively is a dynamic presence and interaction that is inviting, influential, and creates an impact every time.

The CCTA Body Language Success Pillars gives us the power to reflect interest, create connections, and make a difference in people's lives.

But here is the key factor: if you are waiting for a reaction, you are too late!

How you present yourself is the permission you give others of how they can interact with you and is the invitation of how they can participate in your life. Learning to show up proactively can attract more business and create more authentic connections in relationships before a word has been spoken.

The Body Language Strategy System mantra is what you reflect out is what is reflected back to you. The CCTA Body Language Success Pillars are the key to making that happen.

Embrace your empathetic human nature and reflect out what you want to see back first. This resonates deeply in all of us no matter race, creed, or faith. It brings us back to connecting where we need it the most … human to human.

Learn more at: https://kerstinoshields.com

KERSTIN O'SHIELDS

The communication medium for all of us is our bodies and 80% of that communication is nonverbal. Most people spend time thinking about what they are going to say ... but what are you saying when you are not saying anything at all? With 30 years of training and performing in theater and opera, Kerstin O'Shields has acquired an in-depth knowledge of all levels of communication. Kerstin brings her unique skills, talents, and understanding of non-verbal communication to life.

Kerstin is the Founder of The Body Language Strategy Professional Development System, a training system for learning to communicate leadership and executive presence through enhanced body language and expression, messaging, and leadership skills. Kerstin works with international speakers, bestselling authors, real estate professionals, and business executives in Fortune 500 companies. She speaks and trains internationally on Body Language Strategy for Business and has performed keynote speeches and workshops for organizations such as Google, eBay, National Women's Council of Realtors, and the Miss Washington Program.

C.R.E.A.T.E.

Catalyst • Reality • Empower • Action • Transforming • Every Day

JAMES DENTLEY

I have experienced many failures, setbacks, disappointments, and even loss in my life. This is why I have succeeded in business and in life. The challenges have shaped me, built me, and forged me. "I have failed, that's why I succeed!" Michael Jordan.

Michael Jordan was cut from his high school basketball team; Colonel Harland Sanders was rejected over 1,000 times. Throughout history, there have been scores of achievers that have overcome massive setbacks, disappointments, and failures and had massive success. There is one thing that they all have in common. They created a new reality. To live the life you expect, desire, and even dream of you must create it!

The word create is defined as; to bring something into existence. Or, to cause something to happen. I have defined the word CREATE in this way:

Catalyst means to make something happen! You can choose to become the catalyst in your life! You can precipitate the events in your life when you decide each day that you will show up for your dreams, goals, and values. I believe that you can sometimes tell the future if you're willing to write it. Eighty percent of success comes by showing up! Once you show up, you set the example that begins the coordinated actions of others to achieve a worthy objective.

Reality—you must create your own reality. Most successful people dance to the beat of their own drum. Our reality is shaped by our paradigm, the way we grew up and the habits we developed along the way. Robert Kennedy once said, "Some see the world as it is and ask why? Others see a world that doesn't exist and ask, why no?" Most people suffer from a poverty of imagination. You were born to create!

Empower yourself and others! When you wake up each day, take some time for prayer and/or meditation. When you decide to quiet your mind, your body, and your spirit, you can show up every day with a sense of clarity, gratitude, and acceptance. Develop a habit of doing this each day when you rise. Relax in your power. Not a hard loud power, but a quiet intensity that allows you to become inner directed. Lock on to your dreams and goals and be guided by your values. Empowering yourself in this way, empowers those around you.

Action—every day, in every area of your life. Take actions of love toward those you care about and commit to personal and business development. Take action with kindness toward others. Take action toward the pursuit of a worthy goal. Take action and take care of yourself.

Transforming beliefs, actions, and words. The Bible says, "First, be transformed by a renewing of your mind!" I believe you can change your life through the books you read and the people you spend time around. Seek to learn something new that empowers you every day. Gaining knowledge is sometimes like collecting pieces of a puzzle and there's no picture on the box. However, when you get enough pieces, it all begins to make sense and you realize that you have been in a transforming state throughout your journey all along.

Every day, choose to love your life! Trust that even in the tough times, there is a deeper, more powerful purpose in suffering, disappointment, and even in loss. Those troubling times can build you, strengthen you, and prepare you for something even greater that waits for you to turn the corner. OG Mandino wrote, "I will persist and so I will succeed." Focus on getting just 1% better each week and in two years you are 100% better! Every day, write down your goals and measure them. Every day, work on yourself and make it fun! Every day, greet each day with love in your heart. Every day CREATE the life you want.

JAMES DENTLEY

 James Dentley is an entrepreneur, best-selling author of *The 5 Frequencies of High Performance*, philanthropist and one of the nation's top Life and Business Strategists. As one of the world's most renowned motivational speakers, James Dentley is a dynamic personality and highly sought-after resource in business and professional circles for Fortune 500 CEOs, small business owners, nonprofits, and community leaders from all sectors of society looking to expand opportunity. He is also an annual 7-figure earner in the MLM industry and has trained over 80 people to do the same. James Dentley hosts and speaks at events all over the world! He created the #1 speakers and communication program Inspired2Speak: Action Camp in 2008, helping aspiring and established speakers to create a global impact and create the success they desire! His passion is to empower entrepreneurs and business owners to create massive success and to achieve their dreams. James' passion for coaching and mentoring speakers has transformed good speakers to great speakers and great speakers into legendary speakers and communicators. He has spent over two decades working with start-ups of major global brands to help them increase sales, productivity, and overall success. He is an innovator with a remarkable ability to determine and build success plans to help business owners seize immediate market opportunities. For everyone that owns a business or would like to capitalize on their entrepreneurial dream, his message will enlighten them with knowledge and action principles to turn that passion into success!

Produces: JD3TV TV network, a production and entertainment company, radio talk show, and a podcast. He also sponsors high level events such as Limitless for Women, where everything is possible and Inspire2Speak, a business acceleration 3-day event where you are addressed by millionaires and billionaires whose focus is creating success and giving back! His organization, Already Always Amazing, is run by James and his wife, Kara Scott Dentley, who is a powerhouse herself. Together, they commit their efforts to empowering women and bringing services and opportunities to children, veterans, and seniors.

C.R.U.I.S.E.

Courtesy • Respect • Unfailing • In • Service • Excellence

LOU EDWARDS

When I was asked to write a chapter on my "acronym," the first thing I thought of was my title, C.F.O., which in my case stands for Chief FUN Organizer of my company, SpecialEventsAtSea.com.

I'm the guy who got too tall for my hair, started showing up wearing a captain's hat, and accidentally created a brand.

The key words here are "showing up." Woody Allen once said, "80% of success is just showing up." And that I did.

It was January of 2003 when I won a ticket to Armand Morin's first ever "Big Seminar" in Dallas, Texas to learn how to market my new cruise business on this new thing called the internet.

On a break, another attendee called out to me asking if I'd like to do a "JV?" Having never heard that term before, I said, "W-H-A-T?"

She replied, "A JV, you know, a Joint Venture. Would you like to do a Joint Venture?"

Well, it was a bit loud, and I only heard the first word and thought she was looking to smoke a JOINT with me in the bathroom!

I said, "Sorry, I don't do that stuff. I don't really like the smell."

"NO, not a JOINT," she said, " a 'Joint Venture.' Let's go to lunch and I'll explain my idea."

At lunch, she asked if I, being in the cruise business (which I had just started), could arrange a high-level seminar event or conference like the one we were attending. She wondered if instead of meeting in some stuffy hotel conference room, we could have our mastermind meetings on a luxurious ocean liner, in a hot tub on the Lido deck, sipping a pina colada, while sailing away from some exotic, sun drenched island in the Caribbean, Bahamas, or Mexico?

It would have private meeting rooms with A/V, speakers, private parties, networking dinners, group island excursions, even an affiliate program.

Would that be something I could help her with? Having never done anything of the sort, or ever even considering the complexity, skillset, and experience required for such a project, I immediately answered… "SURE, I can help you with that!" Then I paused for a moment, looked her straight in the eye and said, "In fact, that's my SPECIALTY!

"I'm Captain Lou, your CFO—Chief FUN Organizer, and I'll Go Overboard For You and Your Group!" I wasn't faking it till I made it, I was 'living as if,' projecting my future success on our little Joint Venture, and in that moment my business and life were about to change on a dime.

It's easy to create a niche business based on FUN and CAMARADERIE, providing amazing life-changing adventures to like-minded souls who share similar goals, networking and schmoozing while Caribbean Cruising, where profitable deals are done while on vacation and having FUN!

Over the years, I became the "Accidental Joint Venture Millionaire," because I showed up, leaned into an opportunity and, like Forrest Gump running through the world taking action without much regard for the consequences, I was simply TOO STUPID TO FAIL!

Some people are eternal students, thinking they need a lot more knowledge before attaining, or even starting, the next level of success. Not me. Show up. Take action. Run Forrest (uh-Captain Lou) - RUN!

These days I'm best known for the amazing annual Mastermind Vacation known as the Marketers Cruise, with Mike Filsaime, now in its 15th year. I've also partnered with Russell Brunson and Click Funnels, producing their high end Two Comma Club Cruises, as well as Amazon eCommerce, Murder Mysteries, Martial Arts, Dental Conferences at Sea, Real Estate Investor training and more. All on cruise ships, and all because my team and I LIVE my acronym for this chapter.

```
C-R-U-I-S-E

Courtesy
Respect
Unfailing
In
Service
Excellence
```

And did I mention FUN? I think customer satisfaction is the number one priority on the island of relevance. It's more important that your clients know how much you care, than care how much you know. All of this may sound cliche, but under-promise and overdeliver, and clients will stand in line and even submit applications to do business with you.

So, it's taken me 17 years to become an overnight success, going from zero to hero, from Captain WHO? to Captain Lou, the world's leading expert on group Special-Events-At-Sea.

Not bad for an eighth-grade dropout who's never seen the inside of a high school, but went on to lecture at colleges, write 3 books, produce dozens of life-changing mastermind cruise events and speak on stages around the world along-side legendary thought leaders I am privileged to call my peers and friends.

What are the BEST ships? FRIENDships! Sea YOU on the Lido Deck!

Learn more at:

http://MarketersCruise.com
http://SpecialEventsAtSea.com

CAPTAIN LOU EDWARDS

C.F.O. - Chief FUN Organizer

MarketersCriuse.com

SpecialEventsAtSea.com

Author, coach, group cruise event producer and joint venture facilitator, Captain Lou's clients and JV partners (like Mike Filsaime, Russell Brunson, and Jim Edwards) are a who's who of the marketing world's top A-list Illuminati.

Discover how this part time travel planner turned his passion into a 7-figure global online business, without a list, without a plan, or even a clue. All because of the power of ONE accidental joint venture.

He'll show you how profitable deals are done, while on vacation and having fun ... truly living the Internet Lifestyle of success, adventure, and world travel.

F.O.C.U.S.

Follow • One • Course • Until • Successful

BILL WALSH

As we know, for almost all entrepreneurs and small business owners, without focus you're going to find failure, so it's a great acronym to speak about today as FOCUS stands for, Follow One Course Until Successful. So, the questions would be, how do we find focus? How do we stay in focus? How do we realize whether we're out of focus?

A nation without vision will perish. The same thing happens for a small business. You can have the vision, but the vision with lack of focus is going to make it easy to find alternative paths and I find from most entrepreneurs, when they don't have a clear path, clear purpose, clear vision, failure has a way of showing up at the same time, and so do excuses. Start thinking, as an entrepreneur, how do you find focus? It's about finding focus not about being motivated.

I know for a fact, if you motivate idiots, all you have are motivated idiots. You have to really find focus and really understand where it comes from, because it comes from the inside out. If we have a big enough vision, the vision by itself is what truly drives inspiration. When you're on path and purpose with a clear vision, your friends think you're nuts. People think you're crazy. How does that person make it look so easy? You're going to find when the vision is really aligned with your values and your goals, that vision will pull you to where you're going. All of a sudden, the focus becomes clearer because you're not doing 15 things. I find so many times entrepreneurs are all these different things. This just means we're not doing anything very well.

If you went to an eye doctor and they told you they could cut the grass, paint your house, fix this, fix that, are great at working on your boat, and they're also a Lasik surgeon. You'd be like, you're not touching my eyes. It's the same thing for an entrepreneur. If you're reading this today, I've met people over and over and over and they tell me how they are great at this and great at that and great at all these things at the same time. That's a recipe for failure. It's the same with your business. When we talk about the word focus, what it really means is to be so inspired that it pulls you to where you're going. It's not about being pushed. That is not going to serve you but it's when you are laser focused, when you start to think about how this relates to your life, and your business?

I want you to definitely take a moment to write this down. Whatever you feed grows. Whatever you focus on becomes your reality. So, when I have the opportunity to work with entrepreneurs and share with them some of this insight and wisdom, I have found the most successful ones worldwide are without a doubt the ones that are 100% focused. They don't allow distractions in, and they always move the big rocks first. I would challenge this with your business today. If you will become really clear on getting the big rocks out of the way, getting the big things you don't want to do out of the way, make the tough phone calls right away, do the things you don't want to do, all of a sudden what starts to happen is habits begin to appear.

I know, being in business for 25 years and as a top business coach helping entrepreneurs around the world, I have found consistently that when someone really is on purpose with a clear vision, they're focused because they know where they're going, they own their path.

All distractions are equal. Doesn't matter what it is, all distractions are equal. So, when you're thinking about how you will find focus, you stay away from things in your life that distract you, until the big rocks are done. Once you get the big things out of the way, after 21 days, habits will start to kick in. Your vision is so big that not being focused is actually not an option. This is where the difference is. It's not about trying to get things right; it's about doing it so many times you never get it wrong.

There was a story about a young man that approached Jack Nicklaus and he said, "Jack, I just want to be a great golfer like you," and Jack said, "no you don't." He said, "No, I want to be a great golfer. I want to win the national tours, I want to be a champion, I want to get the checks like you get, and I want to get a green jacket." Jack asked, "Are you willing to hit 500 golf balls today, and in the morning, 500 golf balls, and in the afternoon and then maybe even come back for a night session seven days a week? If you're not going to do that, you're not going to focus on your greatness, especially in this sport. You're never going to make it." As an entrepreneur and as a business owner you've got to think the same thing. If you're not going to focus and follow one course until successful, it's going to be tough because there are too many people out there that will give 110% to really unleash their greatness and step into their absolute passion, purpose, and power and do it from a place where they're not being pushed at all. They are truly being inspired and that is the difference maker for all entrepreneurs. Even the ones that have some success and those that have all the success are the Champions. They are focused and they're unstoppable and they're non-negotiable and they get positioned to win.

I would challenge you today that if your passion is to build something great, if you're serious about making something work in your life, make sure that your vision, your mission, your path and your purpose all line up, and then all of a sudden becoming focused is easy and that's the real secret. It becomes easy and you become unconsciously competent in your space, and everyone says, "Wow, that person is focused," because their vision lines up with their passion, their purpose and their big why. If you're not passionate about it, if you don't believe in it, if it doesn't line up with your mission, if it doesn't line up with your vision, there's no way you're going to be successful.

I hope this was helpful for you. Don't forget ... FOCUS: Follow One Course Until Successful.

Bill Walsh with Powerteam International

BILL WALSH

Bill Walsh is a venture capitalist and is the CEO/Founder of the Success Education/Business coaching firm, Powerteam International. Bill is an accomplished author, speaker, radio personality, and actor who hosts and speaks at events all over the world.

With a passion to empower entrepreneurs and business owners to create massive success, his goal is to help people understand specifically what it takes to build successful companies. He has spent two decades working with start-ups to major global brands increasing sales, productivity, and overall success. He is an innovator with a remarkable ability to determine and dictate success strategies to seize global market opportunities.

In 2005, he formed his own company, Powerteam International, to spread his message to a wider audience. Powerteam International provides success education programs around the world and are designed for individuals, companies, and organizations that are interested in creating even more success. Bill is committed to raising the awareness of entrepreneurs, business owners, and organizations worldwide.

For everyone that owns a business or would like to capitalize on their entrepreneurial dream, his message will enlighten them with knowledge and action principles to turn that passion into success.

Bill has an extensive background in foreign currency trading, real estate development, and building businesses in more than 30 countries. Over the past two decades, his firm has specialized in helping companies launch, grow, and create exponential valuation in the market.

The Rainmaker Summit and WIN University programs offered through Powerteam are designed to assist entrepreneurs in creating the focus, plans, and partnerships required to build multi-million-dollar companies.

G.F.S.

Go • For • Stupid

STEVE SIMS

You'll never get everything you want in life by being smart. Now, don't let that confuse you—it actually makes perfect sense. We aren't talking about being smart in the traditional sense—well, not really. What we're talking about here is being smart and safe, or smart and careful. In other words, going through life only doing what's comfortable, what seems to make logical sense, or what appears attainable. Consider this for a moment: why not navigate your life with an entirely different approach—and Go For Stupid?

Taking risks in life requires moving past the safe, the smart and the sensible. Because that's not exactly a fun way to live. Think of all the excitement you're leaving just lying there on the table. Of course, it's important to have tangible goals, they're necessary to ensure the success of our larger goals. However, moving past the tangible into the grandiose (or, maybe even outrageous) requires risk. It requires brushing aside the negative, the second-guessing and the scary. Most importantly, it requires *not* listening to the inner voice telling you "no way, that can't be done" and making it happen, anyway.

Not every risk comes with a guarantee of success. So what? Accept that, learn from any mistakes made along the way and move right along to the next one. After all, the only way any of us can develop the extent of our potential is facing difficulty and then continuing on. It won't be a straight road – the path to success isn't linear. Your goals don't have to fall into a neat little box, nor do they come with instructions on how to build them. That's where you come in, but you won't be able to do it by not taking chances. You certainly won't be able to do it without making mistakes – that's where true experience comes from.

Regardless of what's on your checklist you have to remember that your desires and your dreams aren't simply handed to you. Going after what you want and taking chances along the way does require a certain level of stupid. There's another word for stupid—ignorance. That is, being ignorant of what anyone else thinks or doesn't approve, ignorant of what obstacles lie ahead, and ignorant of failure. Most of the time it's not the mistakes or failures that we are afraid of –we are afraid of what others will think of them. So, stop overthinking everything. Just get out there and do it; and give yourself permission to make mistakes, and fail, along the way.

Pursue your dreams, not just what you think you can accomplish or what seems the most attainable. My career began as a bricklayer in London, which I didn't enjoy at all. It was a job – a paycheck – but nothing more. The problem was – I *wanted* more. If someone would have told me back then that one day I would be working with Elon Musk or planning an Oscar party for Elton John, I would have probably—no, definitely—laughed. Which is EXACTLY what you want your desires to be—laughable. Sure, I would have laughed in disbelief back then, but I would have been wrong because that's exactly what I went on to do. It didn't happen by accident, either. It happened because I made it happen by pushing for the seemingly ridiculous and surpassing "normal."

While you're at it, do something different as well. Far too many make the mistake of thinking they need to follow another's footsteps to do something great. There's nothing wrong with having role models, just choose different dreams than theirs. Different dreams, and *bigger* dreams – that's where you'll find your greatness. Ask yourself what you believe in, what your heart is in, what do you want so much that you're willing to take a chance and not care what anyone else thinks? Then use that momentum to discover the single reason why you *should*, instead of naming all the reasons you might think you *shouldn't*. And never be afraid of being told "no."

Most of us are taught quite early on that maybe we *can't*. That's what makes it so easy to overthink what we want out of life and, sometimes subconsciously, build our own roadblocks. The negative "what ifs" that swim through the mind are the major predators of the dreaded and regretful "what if" that eventually makes an appearance. Quit asking yourself "but what if this were to happen" and you won't look back one day, when fear of the unknown gave up on your dreams and desires and ask yourself "but what if that HAD happened?"

Get used to being uncomfortable, get used to pushing yourself past the limits, get used to not stopping until you have what you desire — and most importantly forget about normal and Go For Stupid.

Facebook: https://www.facebook.com/groups/stevedsims
IG: https://www.instagram.com/stevedsims
Website: http://stevedsims.com

Join my inner circle – The Sims Distillery - https://simsdistillery.com

STEVE SIMS

Do you know anyone that's worked with Sir Elton John or Elon Musk, sent people down to see the wreck of the Titanic on the seabed, or closed museums in Florence for a private dinner party and then had Andrea Bocelli serenade them while they ate their pasta? You do now.

Quoted as "The Real Life Wizard of Oz" by *Forbes* and *Entrepreneur* magazines, Steve Sims is a best-selling Author with "BLUEFISHING—the art of making things happen," sought-after coach, and a speaker at a variety of networks, groups and associations, as well as the Pentagon and Harvard—twice!

G.R.O.W.T.H.

God First • Resilience • Opportunity • Why • Together • Happiness

REGELINE "GIGI" SABBAT

G- God First

Having God first in our lives matters. We would not have all the issues that we have in society if folks kept God First. - Regeline Eden Sabbat

It is important to keep God First in our lives. And it is also important to understand that He wants to be a part of all areas of our lives. He does not seek for us to be perfect but meets us where we are. God is there to guide us in the direction He needs us to go, in order for Him to fulfill His purpose for our life.

We can create all of the plans that we want, but God knows the plans that He has for us. Therefore, never give up. If there was a delay or a detour on your path toward you reaching for your goals, it is because God caused it to happen for a reason. He has a purpose for your life, and His timing matters. Timing is everything so don't look in the rear-view mirror, only forward.

Always remember, God is with you wherever you go. Joshua 1:9 states, "Haven't I commanded you: be strong and courageous? Do not be afraid or discouraged, for the Lord your God is with you wherever you go."

God wants to be a part of your personal life, and He wants to be a part of your business. Too often individuals forget that God wants to be included in their business, as well as part of your relationships. God does not want you to suffer; He wants to help you and guide you.

A great place to start a relationship with God is the Bible. When we read the Bible, God is speaking to us, and we are building a relationship with him. Therefore, it is important to read it daily. When we get quiet, we can hear Him. And understand if He commands you to do something, then do it. God has a plan for your life. Always keep God First.

R- Resilience

"Maintain a resilient mindset daily." - Regeline Eden Sabbat

It is important to maintain a resilient mindset. That means that no matter what challenge occurs in your life, you are able to bounce back and bounce back quickly. When a major challenge occurs in your life, get back up no matter what happens, because if you stay down it can lead to depression, anxiety, and you can live in fear. Get back up and keep up the good fight no matter what challenge occurs in your life, keep moving forward. As God's Servants, we have a duty to serve his people and we need to maintain a resilient mindset in order to do this. If you ever find yourself in a negative mindset, then you need to shift it into something positive. Maintaining a resilient mindset is how you continue to move forward and grow.

O- Opportunity

"Show up for yourself, because the opportunity is truly in the show up."- Regeline Eden Sabbat

In order to change, you need to continue to learn, because this is how you grow. Too often in our society, folks say, "Well, I learned enough, so that's it," and individuals completely shut their minds from learning more. Individuals might say, "I earned a degree, so I learned enough." No, that is not the case; you must continue to be open minded, and always remain a student first and foremost. It is important to show up for yourself. If there is a place that you want to go to such as a training, conference, workshop, program, event, etc. to continue to grow, then do so, don't wait. Follow your heart and remember you are not alone; God is with you wherever you go. And, if He directs your steps or your path to attend something specific then go, because He led you to cross paths with it for a reason. Always remember, remain a student first and foremost.

W- Why

As you continue to grow in all areas of your life, and you work hard to reach your goals and dreams, always remember why you started in the first place. - Regeline Eden Sabbat

What is your Why? Do you know God's purpose for your life? When you know your why, you are unstoppable. And remember, with God all things are possible. Therefore, set clear and measurable goals and stay focused on them. When you wake up in the morning, remember your why. It should not just be in your mind, but also in your heart daily. When you remember your why daily, you continue to grow.

"Keep going warrior. When you continue to move forward you continue to grow. Leave the past in the past. And always take the positive lesson with you." - Regeline Eden Sabbat

T- Together

We are truly stronger together. - Regeline Eden Sabbat

You can't go far alone. It takes a team to go far so having the right team truly matters. When you have people who understand your vision and your mission, coupled with the plans and purpose God has for your life, then all things are possible.

Always remember, stronger together. There is no "I" in team. When your team has a resilient mindset, then all things are possible, and you grow together.

Never be in a competition with someone else. Focus on your own lane and path. And walk together with others to serve God's people in a positive manner. Stronger together.

H- Happiness

"Happiness is truly within ourselves." - Regeline Eden Sabbat

Self-love and self-care matters. Happiness is truly within ourselves. Don't look for happiness in other places, because you won't find it. You are the child of God, and He is the creator of all things. God wants you to live a life of happiness, but it starts with you.

Remember to be happy, not just when things are great, but also in your darkest moments, find joy in the journey. Gratitude truly matters. Focus on why you started something in the first place, keep moving forward, and stay focused on your goal. Stay focused on God's purpose for your life. Don't let distractions or the naysayers keep you from reaching your goals. Again, all things are possible with God.

The more your cup is filled, then you can continue to help others, but it starts with you having your cup filled first. When you are truly happy, then you can continue to serve others. As leaders, we need to make sure our cup is filled. Growth and happiness intertwine, because when you continue to grow, your happiness continues to grow.

Learn more at: https://www.lifeservicecenterofamericallc.com

and http://www.allmylinks.com/gigisabbat

REGELINE "GIGI" SABBAT

Regeline Sabbat also known as Gigi, is a Motivational Keynote Speaker, 2x Best-selling Author of the *Walk With Me* and *God First* books that have been endorsed by Les Brown, and is a Life Coach and Confidence Coach. She is a first generation Haitian American, Financial Expert, Florida Chapter Leader for World Women Conference & Awards, the host of Walk With Me Podcast on JRQTV, Domestic Violence Advocate, Sexual Assault Advocate, Breast Cancer Advocate, Human Trafficking Advocate, and Mental Health Advocate, etc. She is an experienced leader who has adopted a conservative approach to help Christians grow spiritually, financially, professionally and/or personally. She does this by setting clear and measurable goals for those who are ready to take action and experience life growth and transformation. She also helps people get unstuck financially. As far as focusing and transformation goes, Regeline truly believes multi-skilled individuals make great leaders. It's not about focusing on so many things at once, but it is about utilizing all of your skills for the greater good and overall fulfilling God's purpose for our lives and to serve His people.

G.U.S.

God • Universe • Spirit

SHANNON PARSONS

Not many people can say that when they pray, they think of a mouse. Not just any mouse, however. Do you remember Gus Gus, the feisty little mouse from Cinderella? Gus Gus lived his life to the fullest – physically, spiritually, and wholeheartedly. So, what does that have to do with prayer?

Growing up in a religious household, I was always taught that God was to be feared. Out of respect, of course, but it was a concept that just didn't resonate with me. I couldn't put my finger on it at first, but then one day it came to me: *there has to be more to it.* Being taught to be God-fearing is limiting in its message. When I was younger, every time I prayed, I focused on what was lacking and the feelings that I probably didn't deserve, or would ever receive, that which I desired.

One day as I sat in contemplation, I knew I wanted to pray to something more, something that encompassed the expansion I was feeling. And that's when it came to me – G.U.S. God, Universe, Spirit. Suddenly, everything began to make sense. When we think of prayer, we think of it in terms of asking for something, tangible or otherwise. If we expand the concept and include ourselves in the process, the outcome is vastly different. Our exposure is different.

Including the Universe in prayer casts a wider net, but also puts us front and center in the idea of prayer. Nearly everyone is familiar with the Law of Attraction. For those who aren't or are fuzzy on the concept, the Law of Attraction promotes the truth that like attracts like. Positive thoughts affect positive change, and vice versa. This concept certainly isn't a new way of thinking. In fact, it can be traced back to the 19th century when a movement known as New Thought originated. The basis of the New Thought movement began with the idea that most illness was a matter of the mind. Positive thought was believed to play a major role in overcoming ailments and restoring health.

We are all made of energy – positive and negative. Energy, of any source, produces vibrations. The vibrations our energy sends are designed to attract vibrations from another source – but they need to match. Putting positive vibrations in the hands of the Universe is how we attract positive things to our lives. If happiness is what we are asking from the Universe, we must start by *tuning into* the feeling that we are happy, envisioning what that happiness looks like, what it feels like, and putting those positive vibrations and energy into the Universe.

This is where we come in. Now, simply asking or thinking about what we want or deserve isn't enough. If we want love or happiness in our lives, we must shift our thoughts away from the negative and tell ourselves that we *deserve* happiness and love and become a happy and loving person. If we want to achieve success in our careers, we can't simply sit back and envision the success we desire after putting positive vibrations into the Universe. We also must work and take action toward what we want to accomplish.

The opposite of this is, of course, negative energy and vibrations. Those are out there, too, and we do put them there. It's not always intentional. Bad things will still happen, what matters is how we handle them. When negative vibrations find us, it's up to us to turn them around. While it's not always easy to do, they must be met with grace and a positive attitude knowing that we can shift them.

Let's talk about Spirit. Think of Spirit in terms of the whole being – mind, body, and soul. It's the link between the Universe and God, or higher being, and us. It's also what gives us our power, strength, and life. We are all spiritual beings living in the physical realm. And we all have a purpose for being here.

In Greek and Latin, the word spirit means breath, or wind. Just as we need breath to sustain life, so do we need Spirit—it is the core of who we are and how we receive and accomplish all we deserve and desire. Spirit is also our lifeline to what we might call God and the Universe. It's our guiding force and how we express ourselves and experience life. Our Spirit truly is the deepest part of our being.

Spirit acts much like a receptor of the energy and vibrations we manifest in the Universe and is how those are communicated to God, a higher being, and really our higher self. We achieve self-awareness and understanding through our Spirit and are able to be in touch with our intellect, emotions, and passions.

Asking for guidance, help, or changes in our lives really is about something so much bigger than us. We need the combination of G.U.S. – God, Universe, Spirit – to live like Gus Gus the mouse did: being our best selves physically, spiritually, and wholeheartedly.

SHANNON PARSONS

 Shannon Parsons is an empathetic leader whose experience is a unique blend of transformational leadership mixed with a delivery mechanism of heart-centered structure. As a Transformational Coach and Facilitator, Shannon has partnered with some of the largest organizations in the world as a Speaker, Facilitator, and Trainer to Executives, Entrepreneurs, and Business Organizations who need to level up their expertise. Known fondly by senior executives as "The Secret Weapon," Shannon is often behind the scenes and on the stage as a key emcee and host. Most recently, Shannon launched Secret Knock Women, an event dedicated to focus on true women's empowerment and positive growth.

H.O.P.E.

Honor • Openness • Persevering • Encouraging

The Four Habits of Hope

SUSAN ZIMMERMAN

A good acronym has the power to be therapeutic and encourage healthy movement through life's challenges. Its word flow often creates a comforting motivation or a meaningful insight. All that's required is attention and an open heart with a desire to honor our journeys and be open to what they're teaching us, rather than deny them.

Life has a way of taking us into transitions that are brimming with challenges at times. It may range from changes in career, to health, to family. With such changes, along with loss of loved ones, we can almost feel hope melting away like ice cream on a blistering hot day.

But even more important than preventing hope from melting away, it's vital that we mindfully generate fresh hope. When we're struggling due to difficult transitions, it's profoundly helpful to keep this acronym in mind: **HOPE!**

Why? Because it helps us remember the four habits of **H.O.P.E.** for healthy coping:

1. **H** - Honor feelings that emerge and respect what they're teaching us.

Every loss experience deserves acknowledgement and validation to help ease the way. This doesn't mean we permanently deny feelings, give up, or give in to painful emotions by isolating or withdrawing from important functions of our lives. It does mean that we allow ourselves to feel them, even if they're completely foreign or painfully intense. By allowing them to be felt, they have a more natural cessation point and the capability of providing important insights for our future lives.

2. **O** - **O**penness to new experiences, people, and ways of navigating forward helps bring periods of peacefulness, joyfulness, and yes, hopefulness. When we purposefully remain open to options and resist the temptation to be closed, we have more opportunity for pleasant surprises that elevate our spirits and improve our energy. Openness can lead to laughter, music, creativity, and gratitude. It's indeed an important habit of hope capable of producing positives out of negatives.

3. **P** - Persevering even when we feel like giving up helps us gain trust in our capabilities for overcoming adversity, solving problems, and discovering we can still function even during difficult transitions and losses. Persevere means to persist in anything undertaken in spite of difficulties or obstacles. Think about times you've seen sunrays. What do they have in common? They are all made possible by an obstacle. Obstacles such as mountains, clouds, or trees are all examples of what can make sunrays possible when they block the sun. Think of persevering as your special way of overcoming obstacles to allow the sunrays into your life.

4. **E** - Encouraging ourselves to discover our inner resources helps us take needed actions even when we feel afraid or uncertain. Encourage means to inspire with courage or confidence. The many facets of coping with loss and change require us to take heart. One definition of heart is courage. Courage does not mean the absence of fear. Courage is the determination to do something that we know is difficult. At each phase of transition, the only certainty is uncertainty. It is best to think of

courage and fear as constant companions. Courage is made possible by fear.

When we remember the acronym **HOPE** – Honor - **O**pen - **P**ersevere - **E**ncourage – we find new degrees of trust in our ability to discover new hopes throughout life's many transitions.

The phrase "loved one" typically refers to a special person in our lives. For the purpose of understanding the characteristics of grief that can arise in many life transitions, it's useful to expand "loved one" to include loved elements about our life stages, familiar surroundings or activities, or other favorite things about our lives.

Life transitions inspired several therapeutic poetic verses that are in my book, *Rays of Hope: Lighting the Way in Life's Transitions and Losses*. Studies of MRI's show that poetry lights up the brain the way music does. It enhances self-reflection, insight, and problem solving. A poem about grieving the loss of a loved one may also provide insights into moving through other life transitions. It's helpful to consciously watch for those insights. Visualize courage and fear together when you read and reflect on this poem:

> *The path to courage is blazed by fear,*
> *We can't have one unless the other's near.*
> *With devotion, then, toward each we'll steer,*
> *Embracing both and holding them dear.*

Loss is something we all experience in life, yet most of us have received precious little education about how to grieve significant losses in healthy, helpful ways. Society often pressures us to try and rush past it and attempt to avoid the natural suffering that loss and change entails. Grief is a natural reaction to loss.

Our own suffering may be intensified due to myths about youth, love, success, or materialism. Enlightenment is found in our movement through grief by challenging the myth that we can ignore, control, or opt out of mourning. There is no absolute correct or incorrect way to grieve, but it's important to respect it.

Especially when a loss is sudden or unexpected, attempted resistance to suffering leaves us more poorly equipped to cope. We may discover that, to some extent, we have bought into the belief that painful emotions or circumstances are optional. We mistakenly believe we should be able to escape, rush past, or ignore our pain. But when this is what's practiced, all too often our buried grief may manifest in other ways, including health problems or behaviors that hurt ourselves or those we love the most.

The four habits of HOPE help prevent such unnecessary disharmony and difficulty. It can't eliminate the pain of grief but can help us move through it in healthy ways, while beginning to formulate new hopes for the future.

Recognition of Transitioning

Navigating through transitions in healthy ways can be helped tremendously by journaling about them. To help recognize their primary dimensions, answer these questions:

What is gone?
What remains?
What is possible?

By identifying what's gone, it helps tame the relentless swirl of losses that may continuously reappear, providing a more finite element to them. Next, noticing the positive elements that still remain creates the realization that not all is lost, even though it may feel like it in the moment. Identifying positive possibilities, then, generates a glimmer of relief and optimism about the future. I highly recommend this exercise to help elevate your spirit when change is causing stress, discouragement, or grief. Writing out your responses to the three questions will elicit additional insights about your transitions.

It is helpful to recognize elements of grief during transitions when we are experiencing it and honor the emotions we feel. To understand where you are in your transition, keep these common characteristics in mind.

- Numbness is a natural reaction containing a form of denial that helps us cope in the earliest experience of grief. The shock of loss and change commonly has a numbing effect as our minds and bodies need time to begin preparing to feel subsequent emotions.

- Emotions that emerge vary considerably and can take months or years before being felt. Often the emotional journey brings feelings we've never experienced before in our lives. Their sheer breadth and prevalence are unsettling and difficult. It's important to remember that these emotions, while painful, are most often temporary. Their intensity and frequency typically diminish as we continue our navigation through life.

- Adjusting is what we begin to do as we advance through the emotions of coping with loss and change. It signifies a natural shift in focus with contemplation that allows us to envision the future again. Sometimes the process of adjusting helps us move toward acceptance. This is when we discover we have regained some confidence of our capability for making decisions that integrate changes into our lives.

- Rebuilding is when we take actions to reconstruct our lives after our losses. This can include significant movements such as a change in residence, or smaller actions like rejoining a book club. As we regain clearer thinking and renewed activities, feelings of encouragement tend to return, even though there is a mix of emotions that move back and forth.

The adjustments we make during transitions remind us that we'd never been promised that our familiar comforts couldn't melt away. Yes, like the ice cream on a blistering hot day.

NEW HOPE

It was once a wish, a love, or an aim.
Holding tight didn't assure a forever claim,
To familiar comforts, with nothing changed,
Of never having to be rearranged.
Amidst the turmoil, along came new hope.

Slowly nudging us up the steep slope,
Of coping with loss and changed conditions,
Lighting the way for our new life's transitions.

I'm deeply thankful for the many people who've shared their transition and loss stories with me through the years. They've used the acronym HOPE to help them honor their journeys, remain open, persevere, and find encouragement. Their stories are felt deeply in my heart and have influenced my writing profoundly. My hope is that the *Rays of Hope* messages make a positive difference for readers. We all experience periods of transition and grief throughout our lives and it's a new and unique journey every time.

Hope is always near. When we lose what we thought would be with us forever, perseverance helps us find the gift of our inner courage, bringing us fresh doses of hope. Nature reminds us of the positive power that obstacles present when they block sunlight. Beautiful sunrays emerge that light the way for finding new hope along the way.

Learn more at: https://www.mindfulplanning.com
and http://raysofhope.us

SUSAN ZIMMERMAN

 Susan Zimmerman is a licensed marriage and family therapist and chartered financial consultant who has been helping people navigate life transitions for more than thirty years. In her psychology studies, she specialized in grief, loss, and trauma. She is co-founder of Mindful Asset Planning, a fiduciary firm that guides people to make the most of their financial and human assets. Susan's been called the "Queen of Acronyms" as the creator of hundreds of therapeutic acronyms that provide memorable tips to thrive by, especially during tough times. She is the author of six books and contributing author of four others. They cover many topics, including therapeutic communication, personal and professional growth, financial therapy, psychology, and relationships. Her most recent book helps people navigate challenging changes, titled *Rays of Hope: Lighting the Way in Life's Transitions and Losses*. Jack Canfield, coauthor of the #1 New York Times-bestselling *Chicken Soup for the Soul®* series and *The Success Principles*™ endorsed it, saying, "I love this book. Gift it to yourself or anyone who is suffering through a transition, or feeling stuck or lost, which fits everyone today, given what's going on in the world." Susan has been featured extensively in the media, including *The Wall Street Journal*, *The New York Times*, *The Washington Post*, *Money*, *St. Paul Pioneer Press*, *Kiplinger's*, and *Psychology Today*.

K.I.N.D.

Know • Invest • Nurture • Deliver

CHIP HOPPER

The only consistent characteristic that distinguishes the happiest people from everyone else is the strength of their social relationships. One of the most powerful secrets to a happy, fulfilled life is to surround yourself with relationships that challenge and inspire you.

Fortunately, the ability to build meaningful relationships around you is a skill that can be learned. You can intentionally draw the right people into your life and create a life by design rather than just living a life by chance.

K.I.N.D.

The acronym KIND stands for Know, Invest, Nurture, Deliver. These activities are key to developing meaningful relationships and creating space for those you love to grow into the best versions of themselves. Implementing these habits will enrich your life and the lives of all those you surround yourself with.

K - Know

The K in KIND is for KNOW. To know is to perceive or understand. To understand someone else, we have to be able to listen to them with the intent of hearing them and seeing them, not with the intent of responding to them. It's easy to listen to respond. It takes much more discipline to listen to understand and to listen without our own judgement and bias.

We are at the absolute center of every experience in our lives. We are only able to perceive life through our own lens and our own reality. Our perceptions and beliefs come from our past experiences and emotions and are greatly influenced by where we choose to focus. We are only able to process a small amount of the information that comes at us. We are constantly choosing what we accept as our reality. Where your focus goes, your energy flows.

Most day-to-day conflict is caused by misunderstanding. The more we can actively listen and seek to understand, the less conflict we will have and the more productive the conflict we do have will be.

What are they feeling? What are they perceiving? Why did they choose the actions that they chose?

One of the things that makes us human is our ability to hold two opposing ideas at the same time. This ability makes it possible to hear how someone feels without agreeing with them. However, while it's possible to hear someone without agreeing with them, I don't believe it's possible to truly hear and see another person without it shifting your own perceptions and beliefs.

There are times when my partner's perceptions are vastly different from my own, but, when I truly listen to her and see her, it always shifts my truth from the truth I held before I listened to her. It doesn't mean I always see things her way or shift entirely to her point of view, it simply means my perceptions shift from where they were to a space somewhere in between. It is the same for her.

Empathy is a powerful asset in listening and understanding. Fortunately, it can also be developed. Reading and actively listening are two of the best ways to develop and build empathy and emotional intelligence.

I - Invest

To invest is to devote one's time, effort, or energy to a particular undertaking with the expectation of a worthwhile result. You invest into a relationship with acts of love and service. You can use love supplies as a guide. Love supplies can be verbal, physical, and emotional. Things like voice, touch, feeling, declaring, commitment, and responsibility are all types of love supplies.

The tricky thing about love supplies, like many other things in relationships, is that what matters most is how the other person feels, not your intent. You need to be able to invest into love supplies in a way that makes your partner feel you're investing. If your partner doesn't see or feel your actions are filling their love supplies, then your actions are for you, not for them.

Be conscious in your efforts to fill their love supplies. Some love supplies are easier for us to fill than others. Physical touch is easy for me, but noticing things like haircuts can be more difficult. I make reminders to notice things like haircuts so that I am consciously focusing on all the love supplies.

Investing into filling love supplies is good for us and good for the person we are giving to. It's human nature for us not to do something if we don't believe at some level that the actions we are taking will be worthwhile. Investing into filling love supplies gives love to the receiver, but it also helps us believe there is value in what we're doing. Remember, willingness to receive is just as important as giving. Being gracious and grateful in receiving also fills your partner's love supplies.

N - Nurture

To nurture is to care for and encourage the growth or development of. We often measure love in terms of how we feel about another person or how much it would hurt to lose them. A better measure of love is how our partner feels about themselves when they are around us. Nurturing in love gives others the space to be their best selves and makes them want to be around us because of the love they feel from us.

When we measure love in "how it makes me feel," it can become a measure of fear of how much it would hurt to lose the other person. When we measure love in "how it makes the other person feel," it becomes a measure of helping them grow and a measure of how much we are supporting and nurturing their hopes and dreams. We celebrate them when they succeed, and we comfort and encourage them when they fail.

Remember, true nurturing is not turning someone else into you. What someone else decides is the best version of themselves will likely be different than what you would decide for them. We give positive intent to their actions even if we would have done something else. If we can accept them and love them whatever they choose, then we will find ourselves living happy and fulfilled lives.

D - Deliver

To deliver is to provide (something promised or expected). In relationships, we deliver by making and keeping agreements and commitments. We deliver by choosing the relationship daily and by choosing to live in the present. Giving in a relationship is not 50/50, it's 100/100. If you don't feel like you're putting in the majority of the effort, then you're likely not putting in an equal share. Give without expecting anything in return and you will receive more than you could have ever asked for.

We often talk about things like the seven-year itch, but what would happen if we were constantly mindful of our relationship and approached it with the right mindset. Relationships often start with a, "I'm happy to take out the trash" mindset and end with a, "I was the only one who ever took out the trash" mindset.

As mentioned above, what we focus on grows. Give positive intent, live in gratitude, be mindful of your perceptions and of what information you let in. Pay attention to the culture you are building in your relationship. The brain physically shifts when we are grateful.

Make agreements, make them clear. Keep and honor your agreements and check in with each other on them frequently. Architects draw plans for many more buildings than actually get built. This is a powerful way to approach agreements in relationships as well. Discuss the way different things would look like in your relationship. Build agreements, work through them together, redraw them to better fit both parties, implement and test them, refine them. My partner and I have what we call, base agreements, that set a baseline while still allowing for some fluidity in some situations when discussed beforehand.

If you went into a business partnership without agreements, people would call you crazy. Yet we often go into personal relationships with only a few agreements, if any at all. We enter these relationships with our own beliefs and social norms that we accept so strongly that we don't even realize they aren't universal.

As humans, we like to believe we are consistent in being us, but the truth is we are constantly evolving and changing. Life is a journey where the only thing constant is change. We should allow for our agreements to evolve as we evolve and as our relationships evolve.

Make sure you are delivering on the right things by asking how you're doing. Remember, it's your partner that is the one measuring whether or not you are keeping your agreements, not you. If your partner feels you broke an agreement, then it doesn't matter if you think you didn't. It's important to honor each other's feelings and beliefs even if you disagree. The more clarity you can have in your agreements before the arguments, the better you can work through differences in understanding when they happen.

CHIP HOPPER

 Chip Hopper is The BookJedi and The Super Connector. He collaborates and works with iconic authors and thought leaders, facilitating masterminds, partnering in writing and promoting NYT best-selling books, and putting big names on big stages. He teaches you how to tell your story, build your tribe, and amplify your message to the world to generate massive impact and income. Chip's clients include some of the biggest names in personal development, professional sports, and corporate America. His mission is to connect you with the best ideas, people, and tools to help you become your best self and live your best life. BookJedi is about connecting you with authors and sharing their journey, evolution, disruption, and insights gained through writing. Chip has read a book a week for almost twenty years and believes the knowledge found in books is one of the best ways to learn, connect, and love.

L.E.A.D.

Lionize • Empower • Align • Diversify

DR. ROLANDA SCHMIDT "DR. BO"

Lead with Confidence

There is a plethora of characteristics embodied within an effective manager. One of my favorites is the ability to lead with confidence. "Confident leaders empower others to dynamically ascend." When was the last time you empowered someone to become a confident leader? Managers often wrestle with insecurities shackling their mindset to negativity. This stifles progress, cohesiveness, and productivity. When a dilemma of this magnitude arises, simply L.E.A.D.

Lionize

One of the first things coming to mind when hearing this word is a fierce lion. The animal that's often referred to as the king of jungles. Lions are physically much stronger than most animals in their midst and known for being courageous, fearless, and being extraordinarily strong. Do these characteristics describe you? Depending on how you answered, this could be considered a blessing or a detriment. In the work arena, can you imagine a leader coming into work and being ferocious to everyone around them? This leader may be considered courageous and bold. However, would they be deemed humble? It's perfectly acceptable for a leader to be a savage in acquiring business or in nurturing relationships. Nonetheless, treating people with care and dignity takes precedent.

Ironically, the word lionize is also associated with treating an individual like they're the greatest human in the world. One may liken similar treatment to the perks received by a well-known celebrity. Often, they enjoy being placed at the front of a long event line, receive products that no one else would be able to purchase, and are adored by the masses. How does this correlate to your company or organization? During this unexpected season of uncertainty, managers are scrambling to find ways to engage, amplify, and reward team members. A very simple way to do so is to treat everyone as a celebrity. When this concept is manifested in our personal and professional lives, it creates an abundance of opportunities to lionize others.

Empower

A few techniques a manager can use to empower others is leading with empathy, rather than apathy, discerning the finest qualities of a team, maximizing the combined talents, and infusing a communication driven environment. These attributes are a reminder of when my forever in heaven, 18-year-old son Giovanni acquired his first job. As we were finishing a son-mom date at a movie theater, there was a sign in the lobby sequestering a live interview. Giovanni, affectionately known as Gino, wanted to have an on-the-spot interview. I quickly sought to deter his thought process and asked, "Why don't you go home, change clothes and come back?" Giovanni answered, "Mom, if they don't want to hire me just because I don't have on a suit, then this is not the place I want to work." Surprisingly, 30 minutes later, a big smile engulfed his face as he secured the position. Ironically, the theatre manager walked outside where I was waiting and expressed how impressive Gino's mannerisms, poise, confidence, and skills were. Her ability to amplify him demonstrates an empowerment mentality intended to build team confidence. Managers within all genres can benefit from replicating a benevolent environment and assessing one's empowerment meter by conducting an internal and external audit questionnaire.

If an anonymous survey were given to your organization to decipher levels of empowerment, would 90% of your staff express satisfaction? When was the last time you granted full autonomy to one's team? Do you verbally convey unconditional belief in those who may not believe in themselves? Conducting a weekly internal inventory of these questions can pivot a blind mindset into diaphanous clarity. As we embark upon spring, companies and households relish in symbolic, metaphoric, and literal cleaning. Where foggy glass doors exist, a cleaning solution coupled with paper towels follow. The importance of regular team cleaning is just as important as the task of Spring cleaning.

The ability to empower must be void of conflict and insecurity. While sitting in a team interview, an executive manager listened to the amazing accolades of an applicant. Every aspect was considered including the primary goal of deciphering if the candidate was a good fit for the company. At the end of the day, while the team was assessing who would be the best hire, it was surprising to hear internal insecurities spewed from the lips of the executive manager. She said, "I'm not going to hire this qualified candidate because they might cause me to lose my job with all those degrees and accomplishments." The executive manager had no formal college education and had worked their way up in management after several decades of working at the company. Rather than lead with empowerment, the choice was made to hinder another's professional progress and shortchange the team. This mentality is similar to throwing several crabs with the same capabilities in a bucket and finding none of the crabs will allow the other to get out of the bucket. A confident leader would avoid snatching opportunities and embrace collaboration. There is nothing wrong with manifesting trust in one's team and empowering others while leading from the background.

Align

Seeking to align oneself with a personal mission statement leads to the embodiment of bold confidence. Have you taken the time to create a personal mission statement? Is it placed in a visible location to serve as a daily reminder? In the event you have not developed one, please follow these steps to begin a new journey of self-accountability:

- Grab a plain piece of paper and your favorite pen.
- Sit in silence for a moment. I've found it helpful to pray first.
- Think of 10 words or less that describe your reason for being you at work and home.
- Shape a written personal mission.
- Write the completed mission on four 3 x 5 index cards.
- Place the index cards in visible places as a reminder.

The aforementioned steps are similar to generating a motto and readily shared in an elevator speech. Basically, reciting an explanation of any topic in two minutes or less. A solid mission will articulate the values most important to you. My personal mission is "to be a beacon to every person I encounter." A final step includes aligning oneself daily with the personal mission statement and leading well. Prior to starting your workday ask, "How will (fill in your name) align with my personal mission statement?" Repeat your personalized statement when you wake up and before going to bed. Allowing this positive inclusion to saturate your mind, can prevent formation of a negative committee meeting in your head, seeking to destroy the mental gift of confidence.

If you have an existing personal mission statement, please pat yourself on the back. What a marvelous achievement of declaring your divine purpose in life. Several years ago, my personal mission was to "be a servant leader while transforming lives for God's glory." The statement articulates a clear spiritual direction, yet a few life-changing dilemmas led to the need for mission statement restructuring. Are you in a season of change that requires a written shift? If you're nodding your head yes, please follow the aforesaid self-accountability steps. Consider revisiting a personal mission statement every two years to make certain the goal coincides with the present path you're on in life.

Diversify

In business, the choice to diversify often revolves around economic changes, enhancing operations, or launching new products to consumers. Leading with confidence requires subsidiary steps including assessing cultural, organizational, and personal growth needs. Daily focus on these areas is essential and advantageous. What are some rewards derived from pivoting to a mental and physical space of diversifying?

- Perspectives from numerous confident voices
- Teams with minimal paralyzation by fear
- Implementation of reward and affirmation systems
- Productive and engaged team members

An inconspicuous observation of a popular coffee shop revealed a confident team environment. It was refreshing to see the manager leading with excellence when a team member expressed a customer's disapproval of a sour odor permeating from the drive thru. The manager chose a humble route of personally inspecting the foul smell rather than demand the team member do so. He proceeded to go outside and scrub the area that contained a large amount of spoiled milk. The manager went a step further and separated milk jugs and ensured the garbage bins were secured. What is the likelihood that a team member will be loyal to this manager? On a scale from 1 to 100, the team member would very likely demonstrate one hundred percent loyalty.

It speaks volumes when a manager goes above and beyond protocol and demonstrates humbleness. How often does a manager volunteer to complete a miniscule task intended for a team member? Have you witnessed a leader willing to get their hands dirty when others are unwilling? If so, you were in the presence of a humble and confident manager. These profound qualities coupled with regular attention to personal growth helps a manager revamp strengths and flaws. Change is indeed difficult, yet inevitable. When choosing to diversify the way we lead ourselves and businesses, seek to replicate leaders exuding confidence.

There is no doubt leading with confidence is a solid characteristic of an effective manager. In moments of coping with known and unknown management battles, may we strive to lionize, empower, align, and diversify.

L.E.A.D. dynamically.

DR. ROLANDA SCHMIDT

Dr. Ro Schmidt is an author, management consultant, and international speaker. She is dubbed a "humble servant leader," while using versatility to empower her clients. She also enjoys helping them successfully meet professional and personal goals. Dr. Ro was CEO of a tax accounting firm for 20+ years prior to transitioning into academia for 12 combined years as a business professor at Cardinal Stritch University, St. Catherine University, and the University of Northwestern. She pivots this gamut of skills to her current role as CEO of Truth with Grace Consulting specializing in management consulting for corporations, academic and religious institutions, individuals, and non-profit organizations.

She has been featured in the *Washington Post, New York Times, USA Today*, on MTV, ESPN, and a plethora of radio shows. Dr. Ro's happiness is derived from serving God, spending time with her husband, children, and bonus children. She also serves the elderly population in need and advocates for abused, suicidal, kidnapped, and underprivileged children. Her personal mission is to be a beacon to everyone she encounters. To learn more about her background and books, visit www.drrolanda.com.

L.E.A.P.

Lead with • Enhanced • Acceleration to Reach Your • Peak Performance

COLLEEN BIGGS

We have all heard the phrase to take a L.E.A.P. of faith. But what does that really mean in the big scheme of life? Does it mean that we take careless risks, or lead our lives blindly into the unknown because we have faith in the L.E.A.P.? NO, it does not! I have applied the meaning of what leaping means to me in the above acronym. In my world L.E.A.P. means to Lead with an Enhanced Acceleration to reach your Peak Performance.

You might have caught a glimpse of the cover of the famous book, *The Big Leap*. If you haven't let me describe it for you. There is a small fishbowl of water and a large fishbowl of water. The goldfish has leaped from the small bowl and is in mid-air leaping to the large bowl. For me, this signifies what we all know to be true. If we truly want lasting growth in our lives and in our businesses, we must L.E.A.P. with the faith we have in ourselves that we can make it. That in the newfound "water" exists more opportunities, more abundance, more of EVERYTHING! We are our own safety nets, period!

So why are so many individuals afraid to L.E.A.P.? The lack of desire for growth, or FEAR! Without the desire to grow, change, and become a better version of ourselves, we remain in the same fishbowl that we have created as our reality. We remain stuck, fearful of the outcome! No one wants to be stuck, stagnant, and without change, do they? They are, and they remain blaming outside resources for their current situation.

As entrepreneurs, we cannot focus on what happens to us, we must focus on what is happening for us. Look up every once in a while and reap the benefits of what is happening around you. Those you can meet, those that collaborate with you. Opportunities are endless. If we seek, we shall find. But just like a goldfish, we outgrow our "bowls." Have you heard about the proximity principle? You are the combination of the five people you hang around the most. You most likely have the same net worth, like some of the same foods, enjoy the same activities, etc. This can keep you stuck if you are around those unwilling to grow.

Leaping to the new bowl offers the opportunity for you to meet someone new, put yourself in a new crowd, develop new skills that form into new habits, and take on new leadership roles in your business, career, family, and community. Let's break down L.E.A.P. so we can diminish the fear that sets in whenever we think of doing something that we have never done before.

L is for Lead

The clear definition of leadership is simple, someone is following you. Now think in your life who that someone might be. Who is a raving fan of yours? Who are you leading now in your life? Is it someone at work, someone in your community, a friend, family member, colleague? We are all leaders in some way. It helps to know who you lead now so you can determine who you want to lead in the future. In my mind, I was always a leader. Yet, I wasn't always told that. Early on in my corporate days I was labeled as NOT a leader. I was not given the opportunities to step into that role as a manager or supervisor, I worked on projects by myself, and felt very isolated. Yet, I knew I was a leader in my church as I taught others in class, I was a leader in my family cohesively bringing together my children who suffered divorced parents, sewing the bonds of trust and love. I was a leader in my community and in my children's sports teams as I coordinated who was bringing snacks that week for the children.

Even though others told me I wasn't a leader and didn't recognize me as a leader, I knew deep down I was leading in the important parts of my life at that time. As my career grew, I stepped into leadership roles without asking permission of others. If someone wasn't going to recognize my strong ability to be a leader, I was going to create that for myself. I led hundreds of CEO's, in fact it was over 300 CEO's, in building massively successful businesses, led internal employees to ask for what they wanted in their careers, to fight for themselves, led successful fundraisers and created successful programs within the company that increased employee retention and overall gratitude within the office. Step into the role with grace and be the leader you know you can be.

E is for Enhanced

To enhance means to intensify. Working with my clients is all about intensifying the message. You could introduce yourself and mention that you are a Dr. Or when you meet someone, you could start with being a Dr. of blank, share you have over 40,000 clinical hours and be clear on exactly what problem you solve. I like the intensified approach of that scenario. Be bold and put yourself out there for others to know, like and trust! By sharing who you are, sharing your wisdom and experience, people can relate to you and when they can relate to you, they grow to like you, trust you and even want to work with you as an authority if you can solve their problem. I see too many times that individuals in business do not take the leadership role of themselves and create that authority.

Let's face it. No one out there has ever been you, will ever be you, so there is only one YOU! Leverage all of that, including your degrees, to your advantage of being transparent with others. I'm a first-degree black belt in Taekwondo and have that on my LinkedIn profile. Why, you ask? Because to me it was just as hard if not more difficult than college! I gained so many valuable lessons of breaking through mental blocks, how it feels to have a strong mind and body, and what I'm capable of. I'm not sure of one single college that teaches us those life lessons. Be the authority of you, it works I guarantee it!

A is for Acceleration

If you are like me, you may not be very patient. Now I understand that patience is a virtue, and I wasn't in line the day God handed out that "talent," but it can be practiced. I'm of the mindset to accelerate all that we can. That must be why I enjoy cooking instead of baking. Baking requires exact measurements and A LOT of patience to watch bread rise, beat it back down, then rise again, roll it, and finally cook it. When I cook, I throw ingredients in a cast iron pan (a hot one at that) and whip up something quick! This is the way I enjoy working. You can accelerate the growth of your company by creating power plays and partnerships with others.

Accelerate the growth through additional learning and surrounding yourself with those individuals that fuel your success, not snuff it out! Remember earlier when I talked about who you are surrounding yourself with? A good friend of mine, Carey Conley, recites this following scenario often. Imagine you are speaking on stage, and you see the front row of the audience.

Do you want that front row to be your raving fans, nodding, clapping, cheering, or would you like that front row to be naysayers, frowning, falling asleep from boredom, or worse yet, getting up and walking out of the auditorium? Of course, you want them to be raving fans! So, fill your "front row" in your life with those same people! Don't be afraid to ask others for what you want, ask yourself for what you want and, most importantly, ask God! Figure out what it is that you want in your business and go for it! I did when I built Lead Up for Women from zero to 12,000 community members in just 2 short years!

P is for Peak Performance

We are never done learning or expanding our minds to greater possibilities. If you believe that is true, it is! Every year we need to be focusing on learning, taking inventory of what worked in the past and what is no longer serving you. This is what I do quarterly in my business. I compare where we are at the moment with our goals, are we ahead or behind the timeline we set for the business in the beginning, and how can we accelerate that growth.

Generally, if I'm not operating at my peak potential and my team is not operating at their peak performance then it's nearly impossible to reach such heights. I was a runner at one point in my life. I enjoyed running marathons (okay only one of those) and half marathons. I would pick up a run each month for a 10k, 10 miles, anything that I was able to contribute a donation to and hit the pavement to run free with my thoughts. I remember one particular run when I struggled with side cramps and thoughts of wanting to stop and walk the rest of the way (I had a strict policy for myself, NO STOPPING).

These were real symptoms and happening to my body as I was fighting to complete this Women's 10-mile run in Tempe, AZ. However, I felt like I had trained and prepared for the run for weeks. I wasn't operating at my Peak Performance at all! This is how I know that I wasn't. The very next run that I did 2 months later looked a lot different! Between the Women's 10 mile run and the next half marathon I trained harder, ate cleaner, and rested my body when it screamed for it. At the next event, I qualified in the top 40 for the half-marathon for women ages 36-40 and ran the entire course without wanting to stop and zero cramps. How do you know you are operating at your Peak Performance? You are performing better than you were last year, better than last month and even better than yesterday. You are crushing it and loving every second of it!

To learn more about how you can crush it in business to Lead with Enhanced Acceleration to reach your Peak Performance, reach out to me anytime. I'm extremely accessible and want to meet you. We are all in this together, and the more we band together to support each other, lift each other to new heights, the richer we will all be in our lives. Connect with me on social media, LinkedIn, or even track me down on my website, https://www.leadupforwomen.com. Don't allow fear to paralyze you and keep you from taking the L.E.A.P. to your next destination in life! I'll be on the sidelines cheering you on, always!

Connect with me on LinkedIn at
https://www.linkedin.com/in/colleen-biggs-3a22a45/

You can find out more about Lead Up for Women at
https://www.leadupforwomen.com

COLLEEN BIGGS

Colleen Biggs is an Award-Winning Pioneer who empowers women to take the bold steps to Lead Up in their lives and in their businesses by stepping into the spotlight to expand their influence and attract more clients. She has extensive success and experience in Corporate America for over 30 years, consulting over 340 business start-ups, franchising, and voluntary national and local community service. She is an Elite Business Consultant that supports women to move from Surviving in their business to Thriving through strategic wealth building. She is an author of the International Best-Selling Book: *The Anatomy of Accomplishment*. She is an elite podcast host and interviews powerful leaders to inspire, educate and motivate on Lead Up for Women: Speak Up to Lead Up. She has published two Journals on Amazon, and publishes a bi-monthly magazine, *Lead Up for Women*. Colleen leads three successful businesses, Lead Up for Women, L.E.A.P., and Success to Significance! Colleen provides women a community of entrepreneurs that are driven by their passions, to support and promote with a purpose to fuel female voices with power. The Lead Up for Women community boasts tens of thousands of female entrepreneurs that are pioneering the way for women world-wide to dominate the entrepreneurial market.

L.E.A.P.

Learn • Engage • Action • Prosper

THERESA GOSS

Take the L.E.A.P.

Deciding to become an entrepreneur is a pretty big step in your career. Running your own business, including being self-employed, can be full of exciting adventures but it can also be daunting. If done right—which doesn't mean that you won't make mistakes—it can be one of the most rewarding things you do with your life.

Because being an entrepreneur isn't about starting a business just because you can. It's about taking that leap because you believe you have something different to offer the world than what is currently being offered. You believe so strongly in it that you're willing to sacrifice, you're willing to invest, lose sleep, work long hours, and become more vulnerable than you otherwise were. Vulnerability is a huge part of being an entrepreneur.

One of the most inspiring women I've ever had the pleasure of learning from is Brené Brown, a self-described shame researcher at the University of Texas in Austin. She has gone on to become a best-selling author, to have one of the most-watched Ted Talks of all time, and has a popular podcast called *Unlocking Us*. But she said something in her Netflix special, *The Call*

To Courage, that I hope you take with you as you ride on the roller coaster that is entrepreneurship. She said, "Vulnerability is not about winning. It's not about losing. It's having the courage to show up when you can't control the outcome." The same is for entrepreneurship.

So – are you ready to take the LEAP?

Learn

Whether you're just starting out on your journey as an entrepreneur or you've been doing it for over 30 years like me, you will always be learning. In fact, if you ever find that you aren't learning, then you're probably not doing something right. The learning never stops not only when it comes to the practical aspects of entrepreneurship such as learning new systems, new processes or techniques, and learning details about your ideal customer but also when it comes to learning about yourself as a person.

Moreover, there are societal, governmental, technological, and industry-specific changes that are inevitable, and it's part of your job to stay on top of these things. Try not to get yourself overwhelmed and cross each bridge when you come to it. Expect that you will make mistakes along the way – some bigger than others—and this is all a part of the process. Be humble enough to acknowledge your mistakes but smart enough to learn and grow from them. Be kind to yourself along the way by not taking bumps in the road too hard. Being an entrepreneur is not easy! You won't be the first one to make certain mistakes and you will not be the last. Everyone goes through what you're going through.

Engage

Learning is all well and good but if you don't do anything with what you've learned, then you've completely wasted your time. You've got to engage with what you're learning. This means playing an active role in the process whether it's practicing a technique you've learned or trying out a new marketing tool. Often, you'll find that you bounce between the Learning and Engaging phases frequently – and you should. The learning never stops; therefore, the engaging shouldn't, either.

When you engage with the things that you've learned you are preparing to put them into action. This doesn't mean that it becomes a new product or service that you sell or a new tool that you ultimately end up using. It just means that you're testing it out or making a prototype. In some instances, you may be able to put into action something you've learned right away but be careful with this. Often when you're learning new things, you need to run some tests and try it out before you can be absolutely sure that what you've learned can be rolled out with minimal issues.

More often than not, engaging also relates to the interaction with your customers or potential customers. Customers want to know the "man behind the curtain," as it were. They want to feel connected with you as a person. Talk to your customers! E-mail lists are still completely relevant and important to every business that exists, but you should also choose the most appropriate social media channels for your business. If you're running ads on social media and people comment on them, respond to the comments! Don't forget that it's called social media for a reason. It's not enough to just create advertisements or posting on your timelines. You also need to go through your feeds and comment on other people's posts. Not only is this a great and simple way to grow your social media following, but you are also taking baby steps and broadening your brand awareness. You are engaging.

Action

In her book, *Feel the Fear and Do it Anyway*, author Susan Jeffers says, "When we wake up to the potential power within, our impulse is to grab it all 'quick' ... There is no quick. There are quick—and wonderful—seminars, workshops, books, and audios that give you tools, but they are not quick tools. They are to be used and mastered throughout a lifetime." The action phase is about putting to practice what you've mastered after you've spent some time engaging with the things you've learned. This is probably the scariest step—or leap, as it were—in the process. It's scary because this is where we really test our willingness to be vulnerable with the world in ways that people who aren't entrepreneurs may never experience. It's the point where you've decided that the new technique, the new process, the new strategy, the new product or service—whatever you've been engaging with has worked to the point where you can share it more widespread with the world. You are ready to take action. That's not to say that you won't return to the Learn and Engage processes. Remember that those things are continuous. You may learn, after taking action, that there actually needs to be a small tweak in that new process or maybe the technique needs a little more work, at which time, you will go learn and engage again before you put it into action.

As you journey through turning into action everything you've been working on, expect that you're going to run into keyboard warriors, haters, and just down-right mean people. In that Netflix special I mentioned earlier, Brené Brown says, "If you're brave with your life and you choose to live in the arena, then you're going to get your ass kicked. You're going to fall, you're going to fail, you're going to know heartbreak. It's a choice that I make every day. Today, I'll choose courage over comfort." Be brave, my friend. You've got this!

Prosper

In many survival situations, your ability to maintain should not be the measurement of how well you may be doing. Your goal shouldn't be to maintain. Your goal should be to thrive. To prosper. Before getting to this point, you'll want to make a clear definition of what success looks like for you because it's not the same for everyone. If anyone ever tries to define success for you then graciously thank them for their feedback and run for the hills. Some people may measure success based on their balance sheet, while others will measure success based on feedback from clients. Whatever way you choose, make sure this is absolutely clear for yourself so that you can really feel like you're doing what you've set out to do.

Meanwhile, don't forget to celebrate the little achievements—launching your website, making your first sale, developing a new partnership, learning a new process that makes you more efficient, growing your email mailing list or social media following, and so on. It's these little successes that will fuel you on your way to the bigger goals. Prospering—thriving, even—isn't always about making a certain amount of money every month. It's more about recognizing the little successes you achieve as you continually push forward on your journey as an entrepreneur. But then you have to allow yourself to celebrate these little successes, which, oddly enough, can be tough to do sometimes. Prospering is also about not letting up or looking back. After two years, you shouldn't be the same person you were when you started because you've been growing.

Taking the LEAP into entrepreneurship is a downright crazy one. You can read all the books about it and get loads of advice but there truly is nothing that can fully prepare you for the experiences that you will no doubt encounter. When things get tough, remind yourself of the reasons you started down this journey to begin with and then, as Brené said, choose courage over comfort and remember that you won't always be able to control the outcome. Another inspiring author and public speaker, Simon Sinek, says that "working hard for something we don't care about is called stress. Working hard for something we love is called passion."

So — take the LEAP and enjoy your journey!

Learn more at: http://tgo.fm/

THERESA GOSS "TGO"
CEO AND EXECUTIVE PRODUCER, MELROSE 11 LLC

TGo helps Action Takers Bootstrap their way to Freedom from their 9 to 5 Quickly. She's a proud US Navy Veteran who's "earned" a PhD. from the Entrepreneurial School of Hard Knocks. Winner of the ATHENA International TV & Producer Award and inducted into the Nevada Women's Hall of Fame for Entertainment & Media. She started her first business at the age of 10, bootstrapped multiple 6 and 7 figure projects on less than "Shoestring Budgets" and in 2005 published the world's first all digital-interactive magazine for African Americans: *"BIM" Black Insight Magazine.*

Public Speaker, Executive Producer and now National Talk Show Host with more than 2 Million TV monthly viewers and counting, TGo is truly Fueled by Passion, Powered beyond Fear: Letting nothing block her path to Success!

M.A.N.T.R.A.

Moral Leadership • Absolute Inclusion • Nation of Creatives • Total Communication • Radical Innovation • Active Alignment

PAUL SPIERS

A framework for a more purposeful and principled business, 'The MANTRA Principle' stands for: Moral Leadership, Absolute Inclusion, Nation of Creatives, Total Communication, Radical Innovation, and Active Alignment.

There are too many *'vinyl values'* in business: value propositions, motivational statements, business principles and so on, printed on shiny adhesive vinyl and plastered on the walls of offices, meeting rooms and behind company reception desks. While they claim to be everything a company stands for, far too often they end up being a substitute for, rather than a demonstration of, the very values and principles the company professes to hold dear.

There's a very simple reason for this: on their own, *vinyl values* can't lead — or motivate, or encourage, or inspire. And the longer they sit there on the wall, passively whispering to passing employees who have long since stopped noticing they are there at all, the less effective the message is, and crucially, the more disillusioned employees also become.

Why? Because, as we all know, words mean nothing in business if they're not mirrored or led by actions. This is why The New P&L Brand Purpose Institute developed "The MANTRA Principle"—a comprehensive methodology and framework that aims to take a brand's principles, values, and purpose off the walls they reside on and implant them deep in the cultural, operational, and commercial heart of a business.

At The New P&L Brand Purpose Institute, we believe these are the six business-critical components that are the key to a more purposeful, productive and profitable business: *Moral Leadership* that drives *Absolute Inclusion*, that in turn encourages a vibrant *Nation of Creatives*, who are engaged through *Total Communication* and inspired by a commitment to *Radical Innovation*; all of which leads to an *Active Alignment* of the brand's principles and purpose with its productivity and ultimately, profit.

It's no coincidence this framework and methodology is called The MANTRA Principle. The traditional MANTRA is a daily reinforcement of, commitment to, and belief in a set of principles that help you to focus and guide your life—setting a positive foundation and mindset for each day. The New P&L's MANTRA Principle is no different. It also acts as a guide, encouraging a focused and passionate commitment to delivering on all of these core components each day, in every way; helping to set a solid principled foundation in your business for the purpose, productivity and profit it needs to grow and become as successful as you believe it can and should be.

Let's briefly explore each of the core components of The New P&L's MANTRA Principle:

Moral Leadership

There is a very clear and obvious reason why the MANTRA Principle begins with **Moral Leadership**: all positive momentum in business has to start with the leadership. By Moral Leadership, we mean leaders and management teams with the requisite levels of self-awareness, integrity, vision, courage, empathy, and respect for others at the heart of their thinking, their strategies, and their actions. Without this, it's difficult, if not impossible, to demonstrate a genuine, comprehensive and—crucially—consistent commitment to all the other elements of The MANTRA Principle over time.

Like any successful business framework, belief in The MANTRA Principle and a firm commitment and adherence to it needs to be driven from the top if it's to be successfully embraced and adopted across the organization.

Absolute Inclusion

No one has a monopoly on great business sense, commercial creativity, perspective, agility, or ability: no one person, no one position or role (however senior it might be), no one ethnicity, no one gender. Businesses that fail to hire, respect, and give a voice to the widest range of commercial and creative perspectives and life experiences, also fail to recognize the phenomenal cultural value and commercial benefits to be gained from these diverse perspectives.

The commercial landscape is competitive enough today without leaders purposefully or inadvertently narrowing the commercial potential of their businesses on the basis of either wrong or misguided assumptions and thinking, or equally lazy marketing strategies and technologies. **Absolute Inclusion** is where truly diverse perspectives, based on deeply diverse lived experiences deliver dynamic conceptual and creative thinking to help open up exciting new commercial opportunities for business growth.

Nation of Creatives

Creativity and creative thinking are fundamental to innovation, and innovation is fundamental to business growth. Yet too many businesses smother or compartmentalize creativity and creative thinking. The paradox that exists within many businesses today is that while so often leadership looks outwards for creative solutions and answers to the challenges a business faces, many answers and solutions are in the minds of the hidden and frustrated **Nation of Creatives** they already have within the business. The problem is this Nation of Creatives is not being offered the opportunity or the framework to allow their creativity and commercial solutions to flourish. In many businesses, this big, diverse, hungry **Nation of Creatives** is just waiting for the opportunity to be engaged, to be heard, to be creative, to innovate. And because this creativity needs a framework as well as freedom to express itself, The MANTRA Principle has designed a process to deliver both the freedom and the focus a vibrant Nation of Creatives needs. It helps businesses first release some of the incredible creativity that far too often sits far too quietly across the organization; and then provides a process to positively harness and drive forward those abundant and creative ideas to align them with a company's commercial ambitions.

Total Communication

The fundamental difference between talking and communicating is significantly understated and underrated in business. Too many great leaders, great reputations and great products are let down by a company's inability to communicate to its employees, customers and other stakeholders with genuine self-awareness, authenticity, clarity, and inspiration. So often the difference between what the communicator believes they have "expressed" and what has been "understood" by the recipient leads to significant breakdowns in business relationships over time, creating distrust, disengagement and ultimately, an underperforming brand that fails to live up to its promise. The MANTRA Principle's **Total Communication** module is focused on working with management teams and key stakeholders to refocus their communication strategies, approaches and vision, turning monologues into dialogues and keeping businesses and leadership teams focused on producing and clearly communicating information of value, not volume.

Radical Innovation

There is no question that radical, exciting innovation comes from more diverse and more creative input led by a leadership team that promotes inclusion, collaboration, respect, and a deep understanding of the value of curiosity in the innovation process. **Radical Innovation** is not always the most obvious, the most ground-breaking or the 'loudest' innovation. Often, the most impactful innovation over time comes from a commitment to small but profound incremental changes, starting with radical thinking first:

questioning your assumptions, the real nature of the challenge, the real value of the proposed solution and the unintended consequences of it.

The MANTRA Principle offers a framework to help businesses rethink and re-evaluate their innovation strategies and process, including how to join the dots between a company's vision, its purpose and its product or service innovation in more productive, intelligent, and effective ways.

Active Alignment

The final critical component of The MANTRA Principle, **Active Alignment,** encourages the cultural cultivation of all the other components. It achieves this through building a framework for the committed ownership and consistent embedding of the MANTRA Principles into the strategic, commercial and operational arteries of a business, each week, each month and each year; driven by sheer weight and power of the purpose and principles that sit at the heart of the organization. Above all, The MANTRA Principle's **Active Alignment** requires self-aware, self-critical, and authentic leadership. Leaders who recognize it will not always be smooth sailing but who have the courage, vision, and determination to lead real, positive, and long-lasting change in their organizations. Leaders who are firmly forward-focused and determined to build a purposeful business for the future, not constantly looking over their shoulders for what could have been. These are the future leaders of business and the leaders who define The MANTRA Principle.

From Vinyl to Virtuous Values

A business is never static. It's *always* either growing or declining. It's either continuing to build toward more resilient and dynamic productivity, purpose, and profit, or is slowly or quickly slipping away from these. There is no middle ground – if a business is not clearly moving forward, it is definitely going backward, its leaders just may not recognize it yet. Every business has its moments of great success and its challenging times. A great business leader is defined by their ability to be aware and honest enough to recognize where their business sits on this spectrum at any given time, and what they need to continue to either steer their business forward at speed or navigate it successfully through the storm and back to more productive waters.

At The New P&L Brand Purpose Institute, we passionately believe a business that is more actively aligned with the values that define it and the purpose that drives it and has a leadership team that has clarity of vision and is courageous, focused, and empathetic, is one that has placed itself in a powerful position to firmly determine its own successful future.

To rediscover, redefine, and realign your brand's purpose, vision and values and integrate The MANTRA Principle into your business, email:

Paul@principlesandleadership.com

or visit www.principlesandleadership.com

PAUL SPIERS

Founder of The New P&L—Brand Purpose Institute & Host of The New P&L—Principles & Leadership in Business podcast series, Paul is a consultant, speaker and author on topics and trends around Principles and Leadership, Commercial Creativity, and Innovation. Paul believes in "The New P&L" for business. One that is focused as much on "Principles & Leadership" as it is on "Profit & Loss:" as if a business's Principles are right and aligned with its purpose, and its Leadership has clarity of vision and is focused and empathetic, then it will be in profit and not in loss in many ways.

After a career as senior executive in the creative, marketing, business strategy, and reputation management sectors, a life-changing series of events led Paul to re-evaluate where he was heading professionally and the core principles and leadership characteristics that underpin business today. As a result, in 2019 he launched "The New P&L" podcast series and The New P&L Brand Purpose Institute.

Paul challenges his podcast guests and corporate clients to think deeply and strategically on the issues and opportunities around principles and leadership in business and how they, as leaders, can work toward building more principled, productive, collaborative, and successful businesses – those with great, inspirational leaders and passionate, motivated teams.

M.S.G.

Mindset • Skillset • Get Off Your Asset!

SALLIE WAGNER

Have you experienced change in your life? Dramatic change like births, deaths, marriage, divorce, and job change. And less dramatic, but no less significant change, like life creep, when you wake up one day and wonder what happened with your life?

Have you ever thought, "If only?"

Have you ever asked yourself, "What if?"

Have you ever felt that you aren't really living your own life, the life that is intended for you? And you long to make a change?

Guess what?

MSG is your shortcut to change. Your accelerator to begin to live the life that makes you come alive. The three simple steps of MSG will accelerate you on the path to achieve your goals and get the results you want in life, and also strengthen you to face and create your own future, the future of your own choosing. So you can live the life that makes you come alive!

It all starts with MSG. MSG stands for Mindset, Skillset, and Get Off Your Asset! Mindset isn't just thinking happy thoughts, like in Peter Pan. Mindset isn't mindless optimism, pretending that your circumstances don't exist or that they're not real.

There's much more to it than that, and at the same time, something altogether different from that sort of optimism. Because optimism can be misleading and self-sabotaging. When you're scouring the horizon for that optimistic, magical solution, the next big thing, the next big revelation, that Road to Damascus Moment, you set yourself up for disappointment and disillusionment. And, because that distracts you from the real work that's required to get the results you want in life, ultimately it can lead to inaction on your part. Instead, Mindset requires you to face the reality of what's happening in your life. You have to stare it down. Don't blink!

Ultimately, it comes down to faith. Not necessarily religious faith, although it may be that also. Mindset is realistic faith that you will prevail, regardless of your circumstances. Faith in your ability to persevere, no matter what. Mindset is acknowledging at the most basic, energetic level of your being that faith wins over optimism.

Three steps to help you grow in your realistic faith, which will in turn help you build and strengthen your Mindset, are:

First, focus on your perception, and understand that everything in your life—what you think, believe, do—is based upon your perception, including your perception of yourself. Understand further that your perception may not necessarily be true. Finally, understand that your perception is always incomplete.

In essence, then, your life and the results you have in your life are determined by your perception, which may not be true, and is most certainly incomplete. That is critically important to remember, because your perception either moves you forward or holds you back, depending upon what you tell yourself, again, including what you tell yourself about yourself.

So, ask yourself, what is your perception of yourself? What are you telling yourself about yourself? Depending on what that is, tell yourself a different story about yourself. Right now! Words matter. Thoughts matter. The stories we tell ourselves about ourselves matter. So tell your story in a way that moves you forward, not in a way that holds you back. Remember ... it's not what you don't know that holds you back, it's what you do know that's not true that holds you back.

Next, shift your mental focus to your inner reality. This changes your center of power from your outside circumstances over you, to your inside reality over those circumstances. You're not denying your circumstances, you're simply acknowledging that you are greater than your circumstances.

The circumstances of your life are just events. How you think about those events either gives them power over you or allows you to retain your power over them. Focus on your inside reality to keep your own power.

Third, strengthen your focus by thinking about the results you want, not the results you currently see in your life, and define yourself in relation to those results that you want. Most people think about the wrong thing – they think about their current, external circumstances. They define themselves in relation to those circumstances. They react based on those circumstances, and so they're controlled by those circumstances.

When you're living the life that makes you come alive, you focus on the circumstances you're creating in your life. You define yourself in relation to those new circumstances, which allows you to retain your own power. And so you can respond to your current circumstances, rather than react.

That's Mindset. However, you likely need to take some steps to get the right Mindset.

That's where Skillset comes in. Skillset includes new knowledge. Knowledge of how to change your thinking to have the right Mindset. Remember, most people define themselves by the results they currently see in their lives. Their thoughts, feelings, and actions are determined by those results, which means they get more of the same. And nothing changes.

In order to change your life, you start with the results you want. Define yourself by the results you want, not by the results you currently see in your life. And then take action based on those results that you want. When you do that, everything changes. In other words, start with your goals. That means you need to know how to set the right goals for your life.

There's a definite skill to goal setting. Three guidelines you can use to help you set your goals are:

First – make it big! Like Richard Branson says, if it doesn't scare you, it's too small. You either live by design or by default. So design your life on a grand scale!

Second, ask questions. The right questions. The quality of your life is determined by the quality of the questions you're willing to ask. Ask the hard questions. This is definitely a skill that most of us lack.

Start by asking yourself what makes you come alive!

Not what somebody else wants for you.

Not what somebody else thinks you should do.

Not what you think you should do.

This is the question you must ask yourself—what makes you come alive? Because your goals should represent what you really want. Have you ever not asked a question because you were afraid to hear the answer? People hide in the questions they don't ask. They allow others to hide in the questions they don't ask.

No more hiding. Ask the hard questions.

Questions like ...

Why is a particular thing important to you?

Is it important because you deem it to be worthy of you? Or is it because somebody told you it's important?

And who are you when you're not doing what you do? When you're not being a worker, a business owner, a parent, a child, a spouse, a partner ... Who are you when you're not doing that?

Ask the hard questions, peel away those layers to recover who you are intended to be and discover the life that makes you come alive!

The last guideline for setting goals is, be as specific as possible in stating your goals. If you don't specify, the universe will fill in the blanks and you may not get the results you intend. Remember, words matter. Remember also, the universe has a sense of humor. We've all heard the joke about the guy who wishes for a million bucks and suddenly he's surrounded by deer. Don't be that guy.

That's Mindset and Skillset.

Now, you're ready to take action. It's time to ...

Get off your asset!

Once you identify your goals, you're ready to move forward with them. However, be prepared ... what comes next is what stops most people before they even get started. As they start to manifest a new mindset ... they get stopped by fear. Fear is subtle; it doesn't announce that it's here to kill your dreams.

It says things like ...

How am I going to do that?

I've never done that before ...

Now's not a good time ...

I can't do that ...

Have you heard those voices? Or others? All the reasons and excuses for not doing what you want to do, for not living the life that makes you come alive. In order to change your life, you have to overcome that fear that holds you back. And that takes faith. It all, always, comes down to fear or faith ... and you choose.

It's all about deciding, making a commitment. To and for yourself. It's that decision, that start, that stops most people. So decide. Take action! Use, don't just sit, on your assets.

Commit yourself 100%. Starting with MSG.

Mindset—change your Mindset to one of results.

Skillset—learn and practice the skills that will move you forward in getting the results you want in your life.

Get off your assets—by taking action to bring those results into the landscape of your reality.

You have to take action to achieve your goals. Awareness without action creates nothing. It's true that no amount of action in the world can make up for the wrong mindset. Yet action is still necessary. And the right Mindset will empower you to take the right action and make that 100% commitment—to you!

Mindset, Skillset, Get off your asset. And the greatest of these is Mindset.

So, ask yourself ... where are you with your MSG?

Is it – are you – powerful enough to make that commitment?

What if ... instead of if only? Which leads to a life of regret ...

What if ... you decide?

... you take that first step?

... you live the life that makes you come alive?

No more if only. No more what if.

It all starts with ...

M.
S.
G.

Are you ready?
Take the Quiz and find out What's Next!

https://www.whatsnextquiz.com/0
Learn more at: https://intentionallifecoaching.net

SALLIE WAGNER

 Sallie Wagner is the What's Next Advisor. She owns and operates Intentional Life Coaching, guiding you to identify and get rid of beliefs that hold you back so you can fully embrace life's challenges in order to discover, create and LIVE the life that makes YOU come alive! And LOVE What's Next! A sought-after international speaker, trainer, and life coach, Sallie's workshops and customized coaching programs will inspire you and give you the tools you need to achieve the results you want in business and every other area of your life. Sallie is also a Licensed Attorney in North Carolina, Missouri, and Florida; and a Florida Licensed Real Estate Broker and Real Estate Instructor. She co-owns and operates Brokerage and Compliance Resources, LLC, providing brokerage and compliance consulting services to real estate brokerage companies throughout Florida. She serves approximately 2,000 real estate agents. Last year, they completed over 14,000 transactions, with over $4 Billion in sales volume. She also co-owns and operates Prosperity Real Estate School LLC, providing exceptional Florida real estate educational opportunities throughout the world. In her law career of over 30 years, she has provided legal and real estate services to government, corporate, individual clients, and customers. She has worked in various industries, such as telecommunications, energy/propane supplier, title insurance, and health care.

O.P.E.N.

Open • Permission • Explore • Never Lost

ROB ANGEL

Imagine going out and buying a new bicycle. You found the perfect one, and it has 10 speeds. Now, when you take your new bike out for its first ride how many of those 10 gears do you envision yourself using? All of them, right? Using just one wouldn't be very pleasurable—or make too much sense when there are nine more available. Why then, would you want to live life using just one gear? Much like your new bike, life has many more gears to offer yet far too many people get stuck in first. So here's a different perspective—focus on living life as O.P.E.N. as you possibly can.

OPEN to all things with PERMISSION to be your authentic self as you EXPLORE knowing that you are NEVER LOST.

When you approach life being OPEN to all things, an entirely different world, an entirely new you, unfolds. Stepping aside and allowing new experiences in, is the key that unlocks the door to a world of possibilities. You will never know what, or who, is waiting beyond that closed door until you cast judgement aside and expand the journey that is your life – and open that door. The universe is just waiting to sprinkle your adventures with magic – it's time to let it.

New experiences will involve new challenges. Tackling and overcoming those tests leads to increased confidence. Perseverance inspires creativity – that's where innovative solutions are born and new ways of thinking are formed. New environments with new variables help you to plug into parts of yourself that have been buried under the weight of monotony. You will learn so much about your limits, and your abilities to conquer them.

As you navigate through and create new paths you must remember to give yourself PERMISSION. Not just permission to accept challenges and forge ahead with new journeys, but permission to do so being your most authentic self. It's easy to fall into the trap of only allowing yourself to reveal the "you" you *think* is supposed to be unveiled. How do you think that's going to align with bringing openness into your life? Here's a hint: it won't.

You have an inner voice whose purpose is to guide you forward. Listen to it, it knows. It's also the key to your true self. Allowing vulnerability in, brings authenticity out helping you pursue new voyages and expand your boundaries. That's why it's so crucial to move beyond your everyday roles, or what you feel defines you in your life. Your inner voice knows you better than anyone, but most important, it knows who you *really* are. And it *is* who you really are, the genuinely authentic you, who will switch gears and charge toward new horizons.

It's easy to allow others to put you in a box they think you should be in. Chances are you have no interest in being in that box. So stay out of it! Freeing yourself from the opinions of others—opinions about what you should or shouldn't be—gives you freedom to be who you want to be, who you know you can be. Steve Jobs once said, "You only get one life, why live someone else's dream?" That's what your inner voice is trying to tell you— get out there and live your life, and live it *your* way.

Now you've reached the exciting part: EXPLORATION and your chance to become an active participant in your growth, your ventures and where you choose to put your energy. Exploration is both physical and spiritual. When you explore physically – if you do so with a genuinely open mind – spiritual exploration typically follows naturally. A spiritual journey is simply a journey to understanding self and being heart centered. Allowing yourself to be who you really are is a vital step in discovering your spiritual core freely and honestly.

Opening your life to new experiences, leaping over the barrier into the unknown, leads to renewed appreciation of the world. It also leads to a deeper understanding of yourself and your beliefs. After all, it's those beliefs and guiding principles that give you direction and your life meaning. Remember your new 10-speed bike? Think of your spiritual exploration the same way: we are all multi-dimensional beings so why would anyone explore just one dimension? Delve into all parts of yourself – good and bad – it's the only way to find your authenticity. And then turn yourself loose.

Along the way, your explorations may not go as intended. No matter how much it may feel this way you are NEVER LOST. Plans – regardless of how solid – are susceptible to change. Sometimes you can see the changes on the horizon and other times they drop right in front of you like a big fiery ball. That was most likely the Universe's plan all along; it just wasn't necessarily part of *your* plan.

The journey of life is going to happen as it will, full of surprises (some good, some bad), twists, turns and obstacles. There's no surefire way to predict any of these things so the key is to be profoundly flexible during your journey through life. A concept that is much easier in theory than in practice, adjusting to change is necessary to living a life of being open. When your journey wanders off course, think of it as a chance for a fresh opportunity. Be open, learn from it and forge ahead with your newly broadened mindset.

Rarely does anything happen on the first try. Trial and error are a part of any adventure—and a part of the mystery. They're also part of the fun. Think of it as "nibbling at the edges of discovery." You're taking small bites that will inevitably add up to something much, much greater.

Life holds so many opportunities for exploration, adventure, and growth. Limiting yourself to what you know, what is familiar, is depriving you of countless life-altering experiences, opportunities, and a richer, more fulfilling life. It's never too late to get on that bicycle, shift through those gears and start living your best life: O.P.E.N.

ROB ANGEL

 In 1985, ROB ANGEL was a 26-year-old waiter from Seattle. With no previous experience, no plan, and no money, Angel created the phenomenally successful and iconic board game, Pictionary®. With no manual to consult, he made his own rules by relying on his intuition, hard work, and an unwavering entrepreneurial spirit to build Pictionary into a global powerhouse. Putting together the first 1,000 games by hand in his tiny apartment, Angel mastered all the needed business skills, including sales, marketing, and distribution. In 4 short years and with only 2 employees, Pictionary became the biggest selling board game in the world.

For the next 15 years, Rob shepherded Pictionary to worldwide sales of 38,000,000 games in over 60 countries and 45 languages, representing over $1Billion in sales. In 2001, he sold Pictionary to toy giant Mattel. After the sale, Rob spent his time doing what made him happy, including philanthropy, mentoring, investing, and raising his children.

Recently, Rob released his *Wall Street Journal* Bestselling book, *Game Changer*, an inside look of his journey with Pictionary and is a roadmap to success on his own terms. Rob says, "Sometimes not knowing the rules of the game, improvising, or simply deciding not to follow the rules allows you to innovate and succeed in ways no one previously had, or you even dared dream." Rob hopes to turn his book into a docuseries. Rob's present and continuing journey is one of spiritual and business exploration, and he continues to stay open to whatever adventure and plan the universe has in store for him next.

P.E.G.

Passions • Experiences • Gifts

ALLISON LARSEN

Have you ever been talking with someone online or at an event and all they did was talk about their business?

I remember one time having a call with a man I met at a networking event. I was excited to talk with him and wanted to find out if there was anything we could create together. The only time he could do the call was early in the morning at the exact time I usually made breakfast for my kids. When I set up the call, I explained that I would be preparing a meal as we spoke, but that I would be fully present for our conversation.

At the beginning of our call, we said hi, and since I was scrambling eggs, I put the phone on mute so he wouldn't have to hear the sounds of my fork clinking on the bowl. I was thinking this would only be temporary, but 28 minutes later, I still had the phone on mute! He had been talking the entire time about his business and what he did. I took myself off of mute and told him it was time for me to go.

"Wait," he said, "I would love to have you introduce me to your audience and see if my product is a right fit for them."

I couldn't believe it!

"Do you even know who my audience is?" I asked.

"Well, I think you do something with speaking, but I am not totally sure," he replied.

Needless to say, my answer was no. He had not taken any time to get to know me or what my needs or the needs of my audience were.

One of the biggest factors in whether or not I want to connect with someone, is knowing that they care about me. And one of my biggest networking "secrets" is caring about the people I connect with.

In fact, this secret helped me grow my business from a reach of thousands to a reach of millions in less than a year. I have also been featured on stages and virtual platforms around the world as an expert in the field of networking and connecting.

So, what is the "secret?" How was I able to connect with so many amazing people and grow my business in a way that had people seeking me out to speak on their stages about networking?

Here it is, an acronym I call P.E.G.

When I first meet someone, I always play the P.E.G game.

P - Passions
E - Experiences
G - Gifts

Before I ever start talking about me or what I do, I challenge myself to find out one thing the person I am speaking with is PASSIONATE about, one EXPERIENCE that has led them to be where they are today, and I recognize one GIFT they have, such as their amazing smile or way with making me feel comfortable.

So, how do you find out these three things about someone you just met? Here are some simple and natural questions I use. I might say something like, "Good to meet you. Tell me, what are you PASSIONATE about?"

This usually leads to them sharing what they are doing in their business. I then follow up with a question like, "How did you get into that?" Most of the time this prompts a personal story about an EXPERIENCE they had in their life or business that inspired them and that caused them to do what they are doing in the world.

The gift part is easy. After speaking with someone for a few minutes I will notice a GIFT that they have. Sometimes I recognize that the person I am speaking with has an incredible smile. Other times, as they share their passion and their story it comes out that they are a really caring person.

The great thing is that once I take time to get to know someone and listen to them, they naturally reciprocate and ask me about what I am doing and why I am doing it. Because I have given them my attention and energy, they are so much more interested in who I am.

After I am done speaking with the person, I simply take a moment to make a note in my phone with the person's name followed by the acronym P.E.G. Following "P," I put one word that reminds me what they were passionate about, after the "E," I type a few words that reminds of the experience they shared that has led them to where they are today, and after the "G," I put a couple words to describe a gift I noticed.

Here is an example:

Jon Doe

P - Marketing
E - Being called on stage at Tony Robbins event
G - Service Oriented

What next? Well, when I am sending a follow-up text or email after our conversation, I make it special by pulling out the notes I took and crafting a personalized message.

Here is an example:

Jon,

It was so great to speak with you at the online networking event we attended on Monday. I really was moved by your passion for marketing and helping businesses get their messages out to the world! I loved hearing how the experience of being called up on stage at the Tony Robbins event inspired you and I noticed throughout our conversation that you have a real gift for serving others.

I would love to talk about possibly featuring you on my next online summit and maybe even speaking to your audience as well at the event you mentioned you are holding next month. Are you available tomorrow for a call?

Allison

What I have found is that people are so much more likely to respond to my messages and want to collaborate when they feel seen, heard, and understood. Using P.E.G. to remember and acknowledge specific things makes people feel good and they want to work with people who make them feel good. This goes for potential clients or affiliate partners.

So, remember next time you meet someone to use P.E.G. and you will find that you are much more likely to connect with them in a meaningful way. This often leads to more impact and even income in your business.

Learn more at: http://soulintuition.com

ALLISON LARSEN

 Allison H Larsen is the Author of the book, *Soul Intuition*. She has spoken on hundreds of stages and platforms around the world to intuitive entrepreneurs and individuals.

Allison enjoys working with women and has hosted dozens of women-only events and masterminds over the past decade. She is especially grateful for the opportunity she has had to learn and implement the skills that have helped her navigate hormones, stress and the unique challenges that come with being a woman.

Some of Allison's greatest passions include her relationship with her incredibly handsome husband and her role as a mom, stepmother, and mother-in-law to 10 children.

R.E.S.U.L.T.S.

Responsibility 100% • Energy 100% • Structure • Unstoppable • Leverage • Time • Solution Creator

PAUL FINCK

Maverick RESULTS—When you want a magnitude of success!

®**Maverick RESULTS—When** you realize you need to do things differently than you have in the past to get different results ... When you want real results for your effort ... When you want an abundant ROI (Return on Investment), **You want Maverick Results!** Maverick Results are the over-the-top results that change your life, your world, and the world all around you. Maverick Results encompasses the vision we dare only consider in our wildest fantasies. To even share this vision with another scares us because it is so large. Maverick Results is the vision of our fullest potential, come to life, and all that would manifest when it does. This is the life you were meant to have!

Maverick Results has already been achieved by the top 10% who have faced their fears and gone after their dreams, wants, and desires with passion. The good news is they have left clues as to HOW they have done this. What follows are the lessons discovered by analyzing the clues and laying them out for you here. How can YOU create Maverick Results in your life? It is in the word itself.

M - Maverick Massive Action. Dream of a day when you have all you want. When you do, you imagine what it will take. You imagine the activity you will need to do. And you get busy! The challenge is twofold. One: To get what you want will take MORE effort and MORE perseverance than you think. This means you will need to take more action, MASSIVE action to really achieve the results you want. Two: As Einstein said, "The definition of insanity is continuing to do the same thing over and over again and expecting different results." Thus, you MUST do different actions over and over again to create different results. You MUST do Massively Different Action to create Massively Different Results! *"Action is the foundational key to all success."* **Pablo Picasso**

R - Responsibility 100%. In our world, life tends to move quickly and at any given time, and any given result there are literally thousands of components that came together at that time and place to create a specific result. As such, it is so easy to find someone or something to blame; to use as a scapegoat; to use as a crutch for our own misdoings. WHEN you want true sustainable success, you must acquire the habit of taking 100% responsibility for all that happens. The real beauty in this focus is it puts you FIRMLY in charge. No one else has the power to dictate your life outcome other than you. When you take 100% responsibility, there are no blame games, and no excuses. You now are empowered to create your own destiny. That means giving up all your excuses, all your victim stories, all the reasons why you can't and why you haven't up until now, and all you're blaming of outside circumstances. You have to give them up forever. *"You must take personal responsibility. You cannot change circumstances, the seasons, or the wind, but you can change yourself."* **Jim Rohn**

E - Energy 100%. To accomplish all we are discussing here you will need your energy levels to be at their maximum potential. So how do you keep energy high? Is it nutrition and exercise? Is the secret in routine meditation and self-awareness? Yes, and Yes and all of the above. In addition, it is about **deciding** to have high energy. WHEN you know 100% energy level creates the dream life you are looking for, why wouldn't you decide to play at that level all the time? Decide your body will step up and deliver the energy you need at any given time. In personal and business, no matter what, determine to show up at 100% so you can engage with 100% energy. When you do it is when success happens on all levels. *"The average person puts only 25% of his energy and ability into his work. The world takes off its hat to those who put in more than 50% of their capacity, and stands on its head for those few and far between souls who devote 100%."* **Andrew Carnegie**

S – Structure. Structure in your day, week, month, and year. During my initial consultation with a new client, I create clarity around their goals, vision, and passion. Once we have a clear understanding of where they want to go, I am then able to map out the possible pathway(s) to get there. To stay on the path and to continue down the path at a steady pace, takes dedication, perseverance, and systematic structure to finally reach your destination sometime in the future. Without the structures being designed, implemented, and followed over time, you would easily divert your attention to less important tasks, focus on shiny ball aspects of life that will take you completely off course, or almost worse, become stagnated from fear, laziness, complacency, or outside pressures to keep the status quo. Planning out your day, week, month, and year … hour to hour, day to day, week to week and month to month will keep you on task and moving forward. Systematic Structure of the time available to you in your life will produce the best results and outcome for you. *"Mission defines strategy, and strategy defines structure."* **Peter Drucker**

U – Unstoppable. Unstoppable, as in unstoppable resolve to stay the course. So often I see individuals on track to achieve greatness, with clarity of goals and direction, who are stopped by an obstacle in their path. This obstacle looks to them like it is the largest mountain of all time. As such, it stops them in their tracks. Unfortunately, all too often, it is the equivalent of a molehill, small and inconsequential. The inability to see it as such keeps them from even challenging the validity of the obstacle. They give up and never step into their true power living their best life as their best self. What is the alternative? Step up and step toward the obstacle. As you challenge it fully is when you will see for the first time its true size. Only then will you find the resources and inner power to move past, around or through the obstacle that moments before was the thing stopping you from your dream life. *"There is no scarcity of opportunity to make a living at what you love; there's only scarcity of resolve to make it happen."* **Wayne Dyer**

L – Leverage. Your leveraged processes around time, money, and people is vital to success. If you have been in any seminar on wealth building in the last century, you have heard some form of "The best way to build wealth is leveraging time, money and people." The challenge is most people have not been taught HOW to do this or WHAT it really looks like to do it effectively. The concept gets a ton of "lip service," however it rarely gets implemented. To be highly successful, you must learn **and** implement the key processes to leveraging your time via prioritizing, delegating, and other time management techniques. You must learn the key structures to leverage your money so that it is working for you when you are not. And lastly, you must learn to leverage people by attracting and building an effective team of individuals smarter than you! It is only through the learning and implementation of these processes that you will achieve the results you were placed on this earth to achieve. *"Leverage is the reason some people become rich and others do not become rich. Leverage is Power."* **Robert Kiyosaki**

T – Time. Now I have mentioned time several places in this chapter already. In discussing structuring of time and leveraging time. Now I want to focus your attention on how you value time? Is time important to you? Do you really care about it? We all have 86,400 seconds in a day, seven days a week, 12 months in a year. However, some people create millions and billions, while we struggle to create 5 figures within the same time period. The difference boils down to this one question: are you consciously using your time to its highest and best use? Highly successful people use time effectively and the results prove it. They consciously cherish each second as it passes. Do you? Or do you let the seconds waste away doing empty activities? Or worse yet, let others steal your time from you through enticement to participate in worthless endeavors. If someone were to rob you and steal your money, and other valuable possessions, you would be angry, pissed off, and be ready to chase the perpetrator down and bring him to justice! WHEN you protect your TIME as heavy handedly as you would protect your money, you will have more of both in your life. Value your Time today! *"Time = life; therefore, waste your time and waste of your life, or master your time and master your life."* **Alan Lakein**

S - Solution Creator. To be successful, you must be able to manage challenges as they come up. You must acknowledge that all challenges have solutions that you possibly have not thought of yet. Your ability to create those solutions for yourself, your team, and your clients will determine your success, now and in the future. With this skill set in place, and yes it can be taught, you will more easily find solutions in your life, build business structures and systems that cater to solving the client's needs/wants/desires, and become known as the go-to person with the answers. *"There is a Solution to every Challenge!"* **Paul Finck, The Maverick Millionaire®** Bring Maverick Results into your life and create the life you really want. When you are ready to create Maverick Results, apply the lessons above and book a call with me to take it to another level—time is ticking!

https:///MaverickConsultation.com

PAUL FINCK

 Paul Finck, The Maverick Millionaire®, is one of the foremost authorities in business and personal development today. In his over 3 decades of sales, marketing, and entrepreneurial experience, Paul has moved over $20 million in real estate transactions, sold over $30 million in informational products, and ran over 250 live events. He has coached entrepreneurs and small business owners from around the world to build their business and create an abundant future. He has created success in a multitude of industries, including medical, dental, speaking, coaching, training, publishing, real estate investing, financial world, informational marketing, distribution, and network marketing. Paul's passion for life is also evident in his lifestyle centered on his long-standing relationship with his wife and six children—THREE SETS OF TWINS. When you desire a real difference in your personal or financial world, crave a strategic game plan, look to build a great team, and maximize your results dramatically over the next 12 months, Paul Finck is the Maverick for you.

Paul Finck currently offers coaching to entrepreneurs and small-to-midsize companies on how to double their results, appearing on stages around the world speaking on using unconventional methods to build new businesses, create motivation, eliminate fear, and generate new business. He is available for public, private, and corporate speaking engagements, workshops, and seminars on a wide variety of topics incorporating his **Maverick Difference** philosophy.

S.A.F.E.

See • Accept • Face • Engage

BROOKE HEYM

Have you ever wished you had a safe word for life? A word you could use to pause life, breathe, and process through what is happening before you react in a way that isn't quite what you wanted. In one of my favorite movies, *You've Got Mail*, there's a moment when the lead character, Kathleen Kelley, says she was finally able to say exactly what she wanted to say, exactly when she wanted to say it, and afterwards she felt awful due to it not being kind in the ways she would have normally been.

How would it change your life if you had a pause button to process your feelings before speaking or taking action?

It would have meant a lot to me in my life! Growing up, I was stuck in a cycle of perseverance and reaction, instead of a life of intention and contemplation. Around age eight, my mother remarried. It didn't take long for my new stepfather's relationship with me to turn predatory and sexually abusive. Over the next two decades, I continued to experience sexual abuse and trauma from my stepfather and others. At the age of 29, I found myself sitting in a parking lot after midnight, alone in my car and sobbing. I had just been raped again, even though I had spent the three previous years trying to heal and reinvent myself. At the time, I didn't realize that avoidance was not the same thing as healing.

I kept asking myself, how had I just been raped again? Why was I still experiencing this kind of trauma and attack? Not knowing what to do, I called one of my closest friends. I started telling him what had happened. I was coming up with every excuse in the book for why I shouldn't call the cops and report the rape. He interrupted me mid-sentence and said, "Brookie, are you going to continue to be the victim of your life, or are you going to do something about it?" In that moment, for the first time in my life, I was able to see beyond the trauma I had grown up in. I realized I had a choice in the direction of my own life and where it would go.

With this realization in mind, I started a long journey toward actually healing my thought patterns, choices, and outcomes. I started attending a lot of therapy and counseling groups. I studied the mind and how we think and process information and emotions. I learned how our minds become vigilant at protecting us from being hurt. When we experience trauma, our minds set up measures to be on the lookout for the possibility of further harm. These survival techniques, which I call Trauma Soldiers, are constantly trying to protect us by examining the things that are happening to us and reinforcing responses we feel have kept us safe in the past.

Trauma, pain, and shame are the results of things we've done or things that have been done to us. When we reinforce responses to these feelings through repetition, we train ourselves to have certain reactions to them. After 22 years of experiencing intimacy as a harmful thing that always resulted in pain and self-hatred, my mind and body had learned to see and create this in all of my intimate experiences. To have a different outcome, I had to learn to change my response. I learned how to release my Trauma Soldiers, thanking them for having kept me safe and letting them know they were no longer serving me and were no longer needed.

S.A.F.E. is an acronym for a four-step process I use to help clients release their Trauma Soldiers that are no longer serving them. With practice, the process can be done in as little as 60-90 seconds, depending on the situation. S is for See, A is for Accept, F is for Face, and E is for Engage. To be safe, we must practice SAFE thinking. Using the steps of SAFE, you can create a space of awareness and acceptance for yourself where you can process your emotions in the present and create new responses and outcomes.

SEE. How we perceive and see our own experiences is our reality. When we have emotions come up, we need to be diligent in taking space to see them and feel them. Our bodies will always respond to emotions before our minds engage them. If we want to evolve new reactions, we must train ourselves to start seeing and feeling our body's emotions before we react to them. Where do you feel emotions first? In your throat? In your gut? In your chest? Recognizing where your emotions start, and seeing them before the emotional response kicks in, gives us the ability to breathe into them. Seeing our emotions and breathing into them gives us the chance to go through the rest of the steps of SAFE and change our future. Emotions make us human. Embracing them and experiencing them gives us connection, security, and safety.

ACCEPT. This is one of the most important steps in the SAFE process because this is where most of us have been trained to do the opposite of what gives us power. Most of the time, we judge our emotions. Instead, once we see an emotion or reaction for what it is, we must accept it as it is without judgement. Don't assign value or judgement to the emotion or response. Don't "should" on yourself by excusing it away or shaming the emotion because you believe you "should" be feeling something else. Instead, see it and accept it exactly as it chooses to show up in your body and your life. You are not the only person to have ever felt this way or to have ever had this experience. You are feeling and experiencing what your body needs to experience in this moment, so accept it. Breathe into that space in your body. Really feel the emotion. Take 3-5 deep and intentional breaths. Then allow the emotion to dissipate and release from you. Culturally, we form so much shame around emotions. We are told to "toughen up," or "stop crying," or "don't be sad about..." It takes conscious effort to accept your emotions just as they are, but, in order to change your emotions in the future, you must accept your emotions in the present just as they are. Don't assign stigmas to your emotions. Feeling "sad" is no worse or better than feeling "happy." They are both just emotions.

FACE. It's only after we go through the first two steps that we get to engage our intellect and think about what we are experiencing. Once you have seen the emotion and accepted it, then you can face it. If you start thinking too early, you will separate yourself from the emotion before you accept it and process it. Anyone who has ever been hurt (which is ALL of us, by the way) can become proficient in using logical thinking to understand the feeling to try to protect against it happening again. Remember how I said our minds are really good at deploying trauma soldiers? Thinking and logic can be Trauma Soldiers. They are Trauma Soldiers that are very good at doing their job. Thinking and logic stop emotion and feeling by turning on knowledge instead. Knowledge is important to help us navigate the world, but it is not our knowledge that heals us, it is our feelings that heal us.

Facing our emotions does not mean judging our emotions. It's important to still not assign judgement or shame to the emotion. Instead, use meta feelings to understand the emotion. Meta feelings are how we feel about what we feel. There is no judgement of the feeling being good or bad (if you're sad, you're sad). Using meta feelings, ask yourself, how do I feel about being sad? Face the emotion dead on and look deeper. Why am I feeling this way? Where is the feeling or emotion coming from? Is this something I've processed before? If so, then what do I still have to learn around this feeling and experience? After going through the exploratory feelings, then we get to ask ourselves, is this what I want to feel in the future in situations or circumstances like this one?

If it isn't what you want, then you have a beautiful opportunity to create a new road map for the next time. This is where we get to create different future outcomes to these experiences. Using meta feelings to face the experience, we get to design with intention what is going to happen the next time. Facing the emotion allows you to grow, process, and let go of past traumas. It lets your mind know you're safe and allows you to create new paths and new reactions. This step is where the hard work is done, but the hard work becomes easier with time because we are embracing ourselves and holding space for our own souls. We are creating connection to ourselves, instead of disconnecting from ourselves in shame and judgement.

ENGAGE. The final step is to engage with our soul, our source of love, and wrap ourselves in the beauty of possibility. The future is ours. We get to celebrate engaging in healthy coping mechanisms and effectively processing feelings and traumas, instead of shutting down and staying in old patterns. We get to show ourselves grace and gratitude. Thank yourself for getting this far. Thank your old Trauma Soldiers for fighting so hard for you. Show them genuine love and gratitude for keeping you safe.

You've made it this far and that's important and beautiful. Show yourself love for making it through the process, then engage the plans you made for a different future. Engage in love and gratitude for what you will do next. Engage in kindness for yourself because your future is going to be incredible. You are creating the beautiful life you always wanted, and you are creating it with intention.

You are SAFE.

BROOKE HEYM

 Brooke Heym is the founder and CEO of GFR Enterprises LLC, a coaching, consulting, and cleaning company specializing in relationships and communications, outsourced operations and management, and commercial and residential cleaning. Brooke is an executive operations and business management consultant and a highly sought-after relationship and sexual empowerment coach, helping people build better communication and relationships with themselves, their partners and families, and their co-workers and peers.

Brooke advises and partners with other executives, thought leaders, and communities focused on improving the way we live and work. She is a frequent guest on panels and podcasts discussing entrepreneurship, relationships, communication, and sexual empowerment. Brooke is also a published author. She has twenty years of senior leadership experience in operations, sales, personal development, and market research at companies like Opinion Dynamics, Opinionology / Western Wats Corp, Profluent, Evolve Fitness, Disrupt Normal, and BookJedi. Brooke has developed and led large teams, including leading a team of over a thousand employees across multiple states through a series of expansions. She has experience working in dynamic and growing companies of all sizes, from startups to Fortune 500 companies. Brooke is an adaptable team player and a continuous learner.

Brooke is also passionate about improving community and enjoys creating structured processes to hire and rehabilitate people with criminal records, coordinate and lead meditation groups, volunteer with events and organizations, and perform in orchestras as a tuba player. Brooke was sexually abused for much of her childhood, and the pattern of abuse continued into her adulthood. In her late twenties, Brooke made a choice to take back her power and her life and she has spent more than a decade on a journey of research, growth, and teaching. She has developed courses and content that have benefited people around the world in overcoming trauma, guilt, and shame. Brooke was a Music Performance Major at Snow College.

S.E.R.V.I.C.E.

Smile • Excellence • Responsible • VIP • Impression • Care • Experience

CHRISTOFF J. WEIHMAN

I am a huge fan of acronyms. Acronyms are a fun, easy way to remember words of importance and imbue even deeper meaning to them.

As a part of the Five Star Customer Service training I provide, I often will lead groups to re-write their mission statement and/or their company core values in the form of an acronym. I have found that this is an easier way for Team members to really internalize those values and remember and resonate with what that company stands for.

The acronym that I'd like to share with you and expound upon more deeply is one of my favorite words: SERVICE. I say that, "Our highest calling is to use our gifts in Service to others. The world is waiting for you to heed the call."

I believe that no matter what business or industry one is in, we are all meant to use and share our gifts to Serve others. It took me a while to come to that realization.

I have always been a person focused on service. When I was 19 years old, I went overseas following a call to serve with a non-denominational Christian mission organization. I lived in the Philippines for 10-plus years. Within my first 6 months of arriving in Manila, I learned to read, write, and speak the national language Tagalog, and quickly became pretty fluent.

We lived in a communal house a few blocks down the road from the urban poor in Manila near the slums called squatter zones. It gave me great joy to participate in our mission's medical and feeding programs on a daily basis. It was heartbreaking to see the poverty and the poor sanitation of the area. On the other hand, it was so heartwarming to see the smiles and expressions of gratitude on the faces of the local Filipinos, both young and old, when we visited them.

Service is about giving. Giving of one's time, talent, effort, energy and resources. I studied linguistics at the University in Manila. I loved living in the Philippines. I loved the people, the language, culture, food, and beauty of the country. I got married, and we had two children, Kimberly and Josiah. A couple years later, I learned my second Philippine language, Ilokano, the regional language of the North, and we then moved to the remote regions of the Northern Philippines, lived in a village amongst the local indigenous tribes and taught them literacy—not to read and write English, but rather, to read and write their own language.

I believed in my heart that I would spend the rest of my life in the Philippines. In January 1990 upon returning to the Philippines from a trip home to the U.S., our third child, Matthew Benjamin was born three months premature. He was so tiny, and his internal organs were so underdeveloped that he had to stay in the hospital and spent months in the incubator.

As I mentioned, we were members of a volunteer faith-based mission organization, which meant that we relied upon the contribution of financial supporters in the U.S. for our living expenses. My wife was dealing with her own health issues, I was taking care of our two children and daily visiting our baby in the hospital and there was no time for us to focus on mission work. Since we were no longer doing "ministry," our financial support quickly dried up. We had overwhelming, mounting debt from medical bills, and I knew that I needed to do something.

Living in a foreign country where the local currency is about 1/25th of the United States makes it very difficult for a foreigner like me to become gainfully employed. I spent weeks searching for a job wherein I could work flexible hours which would allow me to take care of our kids and visit the hospital. I was fortunate to get hired at a sales job which required one week of training. Finally, there was hope that I could start earning money to pay our bills.

During the end of the week of training at the sales company, Matthew Benjamin passed away at 5 ½ months old. He had lived all but 3 weeks of his life in the incubator. This event was so devastating to our family. But I had no time to grieve. I needed to get out there and start selling. Selling what, you ask? Encyclopaedia Britannica!

So, I now shifted gears from Service to Sales. Every day, I would ride jeepneys and commuter buses all over Metro-Manila to various upscale neighborhoods and go door to door selling Britannica. Instead of serving the urban poor, I now needed to serve my family earning pesos, as an Americano speaking Tagalog selling a British Encyclopaedia in the Philippines!

I dove headlong into my new role as a salesperson—quite a dramatic change from living in a village with no electricity and no running water to going into very opulent homes of the upper class of the Philippines who valued education and viewed owning a set of Britannica as not only an advantageous tool for their children, but also as a status symbol, as well.

The passing of our son created distance, rather than closeness, between my wife and me. We each dealt with it differently, and it ultimately led to the breakup of our marriage. I had believed that I would spend my whole life in service in the Philippines. Working as a salesperson in the Philippines was not sustainable long term, so I returned back to the United States.

I landed in Los Angeles not knowing what I was going to do next. I had always dreamed of being an actor. I had done plays and dramatic duet acting in high school. When I arrived in Los Angeles, I began "pursuing the dream." While taking acting, improv, and stand-up comedy classes, I did what the majority of actors in Los Angeles do, I started working in hospitality. In fact, people who live in Los Angeles know the joke, when someone says that they're an actor, the other person will reply, "Really? What restaurant do you work at?"

I found myself working not in restaurants but rather in catering companies. For me, it was a job, a way to pay the bills. That is until I got hired to work for Wolfgang Puck Catering and Events. That is where I began to understand what Five Star Service was all about. Wolfgang Puck is one of the original celebrity chefs. He came to the United States from Austria and rose up the ranks of the culinary industry. He made a name for himself with his flagship Beverly Hills restaurant, Spago, serving the famous and elite from around the world.

When I worked at Wolfgang Puck in Hollywood, I began to become a student of Service Excellence. I learned to take pride in the quality of the service and the overall experience I was delivering to our guests. I learned about paying attention to details, about becoming proficient at the basics, how to effectively communicate with guests, how to upsell, how to have a balance between too little and too much attention and so much more.

Even as I was learning, when I think back now, I know that I wasn't great at customer service in the beginning. It takes time to become an expert at anything. It takes time, hours of learning, continual practice, dedication and commitment. I took the servant heart that I developed while serving as a missionary in the Philippines and over time I developed that into a different type of Service, Customer Service. But it's even so much more than that. I eventually came to realize that Service is not just a word related to missionaries or the military. We say "thank you for your service" to our men and women in uniform and rightfully so. However, I believe that there is no job, no position, no role that is more noble than another.

If a person is using their gifts, their talents, their ability, their knowledge, their expertise, sharing their story or doing whatever thing they are great at to benefit and be a channel of blessing to others, then they are in Service.

Speaking of various types of service, my wife, Michelle, has devoted her life to service as a nurse for the past 28 years. For the past 8 years that we've been together, I have had the joy and pleasure of listening to her and learning from her. In fact, parts of the content of my second book, *The Customer Experience*, comes from her experience as a leader in the nursing field. She always seeks to find the way that is beneficial for all involved. She leads and serves with passion, poise, confidence and combines those attributes with the extensive knowledge and expertise she has developed over the years. I am blessed to have a spouse/partner who also is my teacher.

Today, I have the great privilege of Serving by empowering companies and organizations to elevate the quality of the Customer Service they deliver to their clientele, as well as empowering speakers to share their greatness and Serve the world through their voice. This is my gift. This is my Service.

The acronym for SERVICE below is a declaration that I use and lead my groups in stating out loud after we have finished a 5 Star Customer Service Training. My hope is that as you read it (aloud if you like) that it will inspire you to Service Excellence.

SERVICE

S- Smile. Nothing is more disarming or infectious as a sincere, heartfelt SMILE. This Sets the Tone for the Customer.

E- Excellence is My Standard. I Always do Everything in an EXCELLENT manner. I Crush Mediocrity.

R- Responsible. I Am RESPONSIBLE for the Quality of My Customer's Experience. It's on me.

V- VIP. I Greet and Treat Every Customer as if they were a VIP—because they are.

I- Impression. I seek to always make a Positive First IMPRESSION on every Customer, every time. I can greatly Influence that.

C- Care. I have an attitude of CARE and CONCERN for my Customers. I seek to truly Connect with them and not merely treat them as a transaction.

E- Experience. It's all about Creating and Delivering an EXCEPTIONAL EXPERIENCE for my Customers. All the time, Every time. I always Strive to make their Experience Positive, Uplifting & Enjoyable. Period.

This is SERVICE. Period.

Contact links:

http://www.christoffjweihman.com/
https://christoff360.com/
https://ultimatespeakercompetition.com/

For a Free Gift:

The 7 Service Mistakes that are Costing You Money Ebook
Text: 5stars to 66866

CHRISTOFF J. WEIHMAN

Christoff J. Weihman is America's Favorite Five Star Customer Experience Expert. His Passion is Service Excellence.

He is an International Speaker and the Best-Selling Author of two outstanding books on Five Star Customer Service and Hospitality.

Through his Company ASPIRE Enterprises, Christoff inspires, trains, and empowers individuals, companies, and organizations all over the country to elevate the Service they deliver to their clientele. His clients include MGM Resorts International, The Bartenders Union, Kirby, DREAM Hotels, and more.

Christoff lives in Las Vegas with his wife, Michelle, and their four puppies, Lilly, Carly, Bruno, and YetiBoy.

S.M.I.L.E.S.

Seeing • Miracles • Inspiring • Life • Every • Second

KEN "DR. SMILEY" ROCHON, JR., PHD

Miracles happen every day … every second! Are you paying attention? When you pay attention, you can't help but marvel that you are witnessing what was there all the time. Choose and embrace being a force for good, and your energy and smiles will transform your world and ripple to do the same with a world you have never met.

S-eeing is witnessing, and faith is witnessing without seeing. Both require having clarity and openness that you are more powerful than you can imagine. So to imagine you are very powerful is a gift you give yourself and the world. To see and be willing to Shift will allow for an accelerated access to your power you harness, often untapped, labeled 'Love.' When love is unleashed on the world, you become connected to humanity and truth. This allows for massive abundance and joy.

M-iracles are God's gift to let us know He cares, He is watching and wishes to inspire us to be His messenger of Love. And this is a miracle when you consider that all of us are eligible to be this messenger. The one who has made so many mistakes, it would appear that they are out of the running, they have disqualified themselves from being a miracle … but they have just actually proven miracles exist, because against all odds … they chose

Love. Hate was their fuel getting them to disconnect with humanity, then one person touched their heart and soul and relinquished what their meaning of life was … scarcity, fear, and pure drudgery. So yes, miracles happen every second. I have met more ex-cons that have given their life of hate to that of love and are free. They are happy, they are living with purpose, and, most of all, they are creating new miracles.

I-nspiring is simply being human, which is to say being Truth at the most vulnerable level. When we share who we are as humans, we attract love and support. This in itself is inspiring. The most powerful energy force after Love is inspiration, because like Love, it cycles. The more you are inspired, the more you inspire and the more you become inspired by the result of this phenomenon.

L-ife is a choice in how we live it, love it, and use it to make a difference. This is possibly the biggest awakening for people, that their life is what they chose. They chose their abundance, their friends, their work, and ultimately their happiness. So, if this is all chosen, can it be rechosen, or unchosen…? The answer is "Yes!" Because that is also a choice and the proof that what we have or don't have is a continuation of choices that are typically the same choice. So if you are not happy with your life, choose to be happy, choose that you deserve happiness, choose to do things that make you happy. So easy, yet so unbelievable that we have this choice and the power to accept and change whatever we wish. Life is what you make it, so why not make it great … why not make it another miracle?

E-very is the description of consistency and frequency, but ultimately it is the description of integrity and your truth. If you believe every second of your life is miserable, unfortunately, you cannot help but prove to yourself that it is true, and you will indeed be miserable. Every is, therefore, a constant, and we must decide carefully: do we want every day, everyone, everything, everywhere to be a reflection of our belief that life is a miracle filled with as many experiences of love as we are capable of creating? Imagine, that you are creating a miracle every time you smile to everyone you meet and everyone you admire and love. The amount of love and smiles you are emitting become so enormous, and so does your impact on the world and your abundance in life. Because that is the reward for being love EVERY chance and hopefully every second you are alive. And yes, you can be love even when you sleep; in fact, that would be the intention of bringing love to the beginning of your day. Every is the opposite of Not every. Think of the mindset of a homeless person, a businessman, a philanthropist—if they adopt "EVERY second of my life is hopeless," versus "EVERY second of my life is fueled with Hope." This is a shift that is night and day to whether you smile and feel alive.

S-econd in the case of an Olympian is the difference between Gold medal and No medal. So, a second is precious. How many seconds does it take to say, "I Love You!"? And those seconds are the most important seconds in a day. And I would hypothesize they feed the next hour or more.

I cannot go a day without telling my son I love him. I don't want him to ever wonder this … not for a second. Sometimes our life is saved in a split second because we were guided by an angel to catch danger while we were driving, to brake or miss something that would have changed our day and possibly our life forever. This is the power of a second.

As a scientist, I wanted to submit a new mathematical formula for measuring abundance – SPH (Smiles per Hour). I predict the more you focus on S.M.I.L.E.S. (Seeing Miracles Inspire Life Every Second) will increase your SPH (Smiles per Hour), significantly leading to you enjoying your life more.

A child laughs and smiles hundreds of times a day. Some reports indicate numbers like 300 or more smiles a day are emitted from a child. Is it any wonder why they bring so much joy to our lives? Why are they smiling? They are loving life and in a state of wonder. Free of stress and worries.

Consider that you have the same choice to be in a positive state or wonder, free of stress and worry. A wise person shared that if you have a problem and you can solve it, then why worry. If you cannot solve it, again why worry? There is no pathway in life that shows stress and worry will access creativity, power, solutions or anything positive. If you spin problems into opportunities to learn, you will find that you access solutions and all the above. But most important, you become a vessel of positive energy for you and the world. Your SPH increases, and so does your faith, hope, and love for humanity and life.

The interesting connection between abundance and smiles is that they work in harmony to reward you for projecting positivity and love into the world. So, the more you smile, the more smiles you receive. And this will attract positive people into your life and opportunities that will be connected to those positive people. You can imagine how much fun it is to work with positive people, rather than people who are not positive, not grateful, and are possibly impossible to please.

Be cognoscente of how often you are happy, joyous, smiling, and please take the time to account for your abundance by writing down your balances of money, how you rate your fulfillment in your relationships, and anything else you want to improve with the power of this formula to calculate your Smiles per Hour. I promise you will see a correlation to the amount of Smiles you emit to how many you receive to how abundant you become. It is cyclic, efficient, effortless, powerful, and the best experiment that will save your life.

Know that your decrease in smiles over the years has been a result of you being resigned to a new habit of perhaps feeling you don't deserve to smile, or that life has gotten so much more serious. I look forward to you learning again that life is as fun as you want to make it. And the more fun you want to make it, the more fun it will be. Because you are a force that can cause the miracles I refer to in the letter "M" in S.M.I.L.E.S.

Some of us are fortunate to be brought up in a family of encouragement and love; some are not. The interesting thing is whether we embrace this or have to learn it later.

I highly recommend you order "KEEP SMILING" cards that you can put in areas that remind you to be in gratitude and order a lot extra so you can do what my mentor, Barry Shore, taught me … pay it forward and give out two cards to people either needing a smile or reward those who are smiling.

If you give a KEEP SMILING card to someone and they are reminded to be positive, you become a source of that positive energy, and it will connect back to you in so many ways.

It is your choice to AMPLIFY GOODNESS in the world, and if you choose to do this, you will experience how much you matter and you will awaken a purpose for living that will ignite your love of life and those in your life will certainly celebrate this new zeal and zest you have exhibited for the world to be inspired by. And soon you will be sought after for your wisdom in how you created a life you love because you understand how to increase your SPH using the acronym S.M.I.L.E.

Ken "Dr. Smiley" Rochon, Jr., PhD

www.theKEEPSMILINGmovement.com

KEN "DR. SMILEY" ROCHON, JR., PHD

Ken Rochon, Jr., is a renaissance man, humanitarian, and an accomplished serial entrepreneur. He is a social proof celebrity event photographer, international keynote speaker, and published author of 30 books. He has been honored as "America's Most Influential Business Connector" and "Entrepreneur of the Year."

UmbrellaSyndicate.com (a Marketing, Promotion, and Media Company); PerfectPublishing.com (a Book Publishing Company); and AbsoluteEntertainment.com (DJ Company) are a few of his businesses. Ken's focus is supporting causes and non-profits to "Amplifying Leaders Who Lead with Their Heart." His radio show, "Amplified" on Voice America Influencer Channel, is a platform he uses to discuss building community, fatherhood, leadership, success principles, and values. Ken, who lost his mother to Alzheimer's complications, desires to live a life of purpose where he leaves a legacy of love for his son to model. He is the Co-Founder of TheKeepSmilingMovement.com, a non-profit organization . He has published over 110 books of leaders. The movement shares these books with everyone needing a "DOSE of HOPE." His love of the arts and sciences inspired him to travel to over 100 countries. His favorite place to be is with his son, K3, the light of his life.

S.O.S.

Shift Your Focus • Oxygen • Schedule Your Success

JENNIFER J. HAMMOND

Women Who Lead Use S.O.S.

No, I assure you that I am not referring to a distress call! S.O.S. is an acronym that empowers women to take charge of their perspective and their success. Rather than focusing on the obstacles, challenges, and losses, S.O.S. focuses on your success and how to bring out all of the positivity in your life. Before we jump into my version of S.O.S., let's take a quick look at the history of the marine and naval use of S.O.S. – you'll be interested to learn how things have changed!

The History of the Most Famous Acronym

The S.O.S. acronym has been used in many different forms throughout history. You may have even heard international superstar Rihanna use it as the title of one of her hit songs. But the history of S.O.S. is simple and, quite honestly, uneventful – which is why I reclaimed it for a much more exciting purpose!

Many people are under the impression that this acronym stands for *save our ship*. However, the truth is that it actually doesn't stand for anything. This maritime distress call is an evolution of the original acronym, CDQ. The "CQ" part of CDQ was a signal that would send a message to all operators. The "D" was later added to signify a situation of distress.

The original signal was later adopted to S.O.S. because of how simple this signal is to use. In morse code, S is signified by three dots, while O is transmitted by sending three dashes. The straightforward and universally understood nature of the signal was accepted internationally and used by all maritime vessels to let operators know if there was an emergency.

While my version of S.O.S. doesn't signify distress or an emergency, it is simple and straightforward. Even better, everyone can understand how to interpret it and use it for their success. Let's get you acquainted with the new and improved version of S.O.S.

The New S.O.S!

Here is what it stands for:

S – Shift Your Focus
O – Oxygen
S – Schedule Your Success

These three steps will help you direct your efforts and energy toward future accomplishments while focusing on the constructive and optimistic aspects of your life along the way! Too often, we get bogged down by spending too much of our time and energy on our *losses*. Whether it's a personal loss or loss in business, focusing too much on these challenges takes away from our ability to stay focused and motivated to move on and create new wins and successes.

By directing your intentions toward the positives and the wins, you attract the same energy back—that's no secret! However, knowing how to start being more optimistic and positive can be challenging to start. Some of us just aren't sure how to turn our perspective around. S.O.S. is the framework to get you into this state of mind *all of the time*. Let's take a deeper look at each of the steps.

First, **Shift** Your Focus.

The first *S* in S.O.S. stands for *shift your focus*. Before we can make any significant changes and be the great leaders that we were meant to be, we have to align our focus and our vision with success. It is all too common for women to experience a success and quickly dismiss it as we are often taught to be more modest, or we want to keep moving forward to the subsequent successes. However, I want to know why we don't have the same attitude toward our losses? Much too often, we experience a loss or a challenge that we could not overcome at the first attempt, and we spend *so much* time focusing our energy and attention on that loss. The truth is that it already happened and the only thing to do is try to find a lesson from it and keep moving forward.

However, successes are so much richer than losses. Not only can we look at our successes to see what we did right and what worked well to achieve the desired result, but we can also build off of that sense of confidence and accomplishment that came from that success. This is what I mean by shifting your focus. When you're feeling defeated or upset by a perceived loss, take a moment to think about your *wins* or even something that is just silly and funny! By taking that negative energy and repurposing it into something much more positive and optimistic, we are able to continue moving forward – YAY! Women who lead look toward the horizon, the future, and all of the possibility that comes with it, which leaves absolutely no time to spend pondering over the things that didn't work out perfectly.

Find Your YAY In EVERY DAY – **Oxygen**

We as women have a tendency to put everyone else before ourselves, but if you have ever been on a plane, then you know that you have to put on your own oxygen mask first before you can help anyone else. There's a reason that flight attendants instruct you to take care of yourself before helping others. It is because you aren't nearly as helpful when you are struggling and not taking care of yourself as when you are happy, healthy, and thriving.

Women wear many different hats, and we do it *very* well. However, there are many things that we let fall by the wayside so that we can juggle all of our roles—exercise, meditation, eating healthy, getting enough sleep, the list goes on. It is so important that we take care of ourselves so that we can lead teams, our families, board rooms, and anywhere else our skills and vision bring success and progress!

So, when I say put your oxygen mask on first, I mean that you have to prioritize yourself as much as possible. Figure out what makes you feel good and brings the most joy and happiness to your life – that is your YAY! Once you find out what those things are, you need to practice at least some of them every single day, no exceptions! If you feel centered and at peace after a Pilates workout or yoga practice, then start your day with a half-hour session. Do you feel better when you add more fruits and veggies to your day? Fantastic, make sure to get all of your favorites during your next trip to the grocery store and add a few more at every meal!

There is no secret sauce to this step. It is about taking the time to learn what makes you feel great! At first, it can be hard to set aside time for yourself, but once you start carving out parts of your day to take care of *yourself*, then you will see the positive effect it has on every other aspect of your life.

Schedule Your Success

What is one thing all successful female leaders have in common? They take the time and energy to schedule a plan and a path to their success. Women who are successful did not stumble onto their achievements by accident. They prioritized the steps that it would take to accomplish their goals. So, how do you start practicing this step? You figure out what success looks like to you, and then you schedule it!

Here is an example, let's say you want to write a novel. YAY – we love this idea! Novels take a lot of time, energy, and work to complete. Think of all the elements of a novel that you have to figure out—characters, plotlines, metaphors, style, the list will likely feel endless. Without a plan and without setting aside time to work on your book on a consistent basis, I can bet you that you won't finish it. And it won't be because you *can't* finish it, it'll be because you didn't *plan* to finish it.

Rather than setting a goal with the intention of working toward when you have the time, you make the time! So, you want to write that novel? Set aside 30 minutes every day to dedicate to your work! Setting smaller, achievable goals helps you reach the big one at the top of the mountain, but you have to make your success a consistent and daily practice.

Final Thoughts

S.O.S. is as effective as it is simple! Women have so much potential, especially as leaders, which is why it is so important to focus on our ability to lead as well as our successes. When we direct our attention and our time to focusing on the positives, taking care of ourselves, and setting time aside for the things that we love, we create the best possible version of ourselves. That version is a woman who leads a happy and rewarding life while getting things *done!*

Learn more at: www.jenniferjhammond.com

JENNIFER HAMMOND

 Jennifer Hammond is a high energy and versatile woman who not only serves as a real estate executive; but also as a podcast talk show host, a best-selling author, and is a member of The Happiness Hall of Fame! As a Vice President of TTR Sotheby's International Realty—one of the country's leading real estate companies—she has helped hundreds of clients attain their dreams in real estate for over 23 years, has helped make the world a better place by educating, inspiring, and empowering people by hosting The Jennifer Hammond Show on SiriusXM for over 10+ years, and has aided thousands of veterans and their families in finding the help they need through her best-selling book, *101+ Resources for Veterans.*

However, the path to her success was not an easy one. Though she is the granddaughter of a woman who survived concentration camps and is now enshrined in the USA's Baseball Hall of Fame, Jennifer grew up in a broken and abusive home and was repeatedly told she would never amount to anything; and that opinion was further impressed on her when, in high school, she was told by a guidance counselor that she "was not smart enough" to attend college. Nevertheless, determined to make something great of her life, Jennifer never gave up.

Toward the end of her senior year in high school, another guidance counselor informed her that—based on her "potential for greatness"—she was chosen to be the first recipient of the "Tommie Roberts Memorial Scholarship," established in honor of her former Key West High School principal and awarded to "a deserving student to create an opportunity at greatness!"

She went on to attend Florida Keys Community College, where she earned an Associate's Degree, then went on to earn a Bachelor's Degree in Legal Administration from The University of West Florida, where she served as the student body president, and then earned a Master's Degree in Public Administration shortly thereafter.

S.P.A.LIFE

Seek • Power • Always • LIFE: Living in Freedom Epically!

DIANE HALFMAN

S - SEEK ... strength from systems
P - POWER ... within you
A - ALWAYS ... care for yourself
Life: Living In Freedom Epically!

I was a decade into my career as a San Diego Police Officer when I was badly injured in a training accident, forcing me into an early retirement. Within the first year of my retirement, I received word that my friend's seven-year-old daughter was missing. I was asked to be the liaison between the family and the police department in finding her child. It was quickly learned the little girl had been kidnapped. I helped formulate what became the largest volunteer effort in US history to search for her. Timing became critical. Ultimately, it took us three weeks to find her body. She had been kidnapped, sexually assaulted, and then murdered.

This was a life-changing event for many people. It was a very acute experience that taught me how quickly getting my hands on something like a family photo could be critical. This is why I am so adamant about organizing and creating systems. I pray that no one ever has to experience something so traumatic. Having the fortitude to move with grace, through anything that life throws at you, is possible when you have the systems and structures in place.

It was after this kidnapping case that my friend and I went to Canyon Ranch in Tucson. With her daughter gone and family life in shambles, we all needed recovery and soul searching. It was there, in an environment of extreme self-care, that I coined the term SPAlife. It was a journey to discover what that term truly meant to me. It began with looking at all of my environments (people, home, relationships, spirituality, finances, mindset, body) and getting them in alignment with my values.

It evolved into ditching the illusive "balance" to look at SPAlife as a lifestyle that accepts that accomplishment and harmony co-exist with the ebb and flow of life and being guided by my values. I have always trusted my intuition and that saved me countless times in my police work, especially when working undercover investigations.

Later, I began to notice that many of my clients were being influenced by external circumstances. I saw they were giving their power away. I would share that real power doesn't happen outside of you. You are your own power! The SPA in "SPAlife" stands for Seek Power Always—that power within you to do your deeper work in the world.

Below is a further exploration of how SPAlife holds the framework of systems, the foundation of power and the fabric of self-care.

S - SEEK Strength from Systems

Seeking indicates you are on a journey embracing change. It allows you to expand and grow, to be on a path to learn, adapt, and cultivate new skills. Seeking and finding what's important to you empowers you to have a simpler life. Complexity kills so when you keep things simple, your communication is better, your commitments stronger and collaborations smoother.

I have found a simple value-filled life is best supported by having systems.

Systems give you predictable success. Creating positive environments supports your systems. Positive environments are the foundation to rely on your systems in a consistent, dependable way. This allows you to better navigate changes in your priority and all the moving parts of everyday life.

One of my favorite tools is a systematic calendar. I always say, "Your calendar is M.I.A." It can be either your "Mind In Action," where your life is aligned with your values, or your mind becomes "Missing In Action" because you're allowing others to dictate how you spend your time. You'll know which is true for you simply by looking at your calendar!

My client, Matt, loves sailing, yet in the two years of owning a sailboat, had only been on it a few times. I asked him when he planned on using his boat more consistently. He told me, "When I retire." He said he was too busy now, working seven days a week. I asked him if he would trust me to create a calendar system that would align more with the life he wanted to live right now. He agreed, and I said, "Starting next Friday, and every Friday after, you are "retired" on Fridays and the weekends. You have no scheduled appointments, no alarms, and you go sail on Friday. Saturdays are family days and Sundays are to restore yourself."

By agreeing to change how he was doing things and create a system that allowed him to live the life he really wanted, Matt found renewed strength in all aspects of his life. While on the water he had his most creative ideas and the passion to implement them, even while working less.

Is it time for you to seek a different perspective?

P - POWER Within You

I believe that YOU are your own power! Too many people give their power away. There is a distinction between gathering guidance and knowledge from a mentor or friend versus trusting your internal intuition and knowing to make the important decisions for your life.

True positive internal power is harnessed by centering yourself to rely on your connection, consciousness, and contribution to lead you on the noble path that has been created just for you and your unique skills and talents.

To access your power, you must have a core connection with yourself and who you really are. When you connect to the power within, you are unshakable, and you can do anything! Consciousness is a dimmer switch. When your access is high, you are in flow to draw on your power.

My client, Meg, told me that she wasn't stepping fully into her power. She recognized that, unconsciously, she was sabotaging herself by not fully enjoying or being with what she wanted. Meg would accomplish something then feel guilty, overwhelmed, or angry about it. She was a multi-tasking maniac and she longed to be more grounded, consistent, and trusting of herself. She began to feel like she was on the edge of a breakdown and wanted to avoid going into a crisis.

Meg started meditating more consistently and was able to use her breath to slow down enough to hear what her wise, powerful self was telling her. Breathing more consciously is vital because without proper oxygen you can't have cognitive function. If you can't think right, then you are more easily pushed around, controlled, or manipulated. Knowing how to better utilize your breath is a game changer! All of my clients have the tools to go from emotional reactions to calm responding and feeling more confident standing in their power.

Contribution begins with you and what you have to give. Getting centered is supported by knowing your 4 Levels of Power. Mastering your power within gives you access to your unique gifts. One of the favorite tools I created uses breath and asking questions. It's called P.I.E.S., which stands for Physical, Intellectual, Emotional, and Spiritual Power.

Being able to access the divinity within you is tapping into your God-given power. It's not a passive process. You can actively ask God for what you want and listen for the many ways He speaks to you through your internal power and intuition. You just have to listen. The word silent has the same letters as listen and they go hand in hand. The verse "Be still and know that I am God" is a practice of silence where you listen to God's messages for you.

Questions help you get clear on what you want faster and with ease. You will have better access to your wisdom and common sense. You will develop the ability to trust without second guessing yourself and handle situations with both vulnerability and courage.

Isn't it time to access the real true power within yourself?!

A - ALWAYS Care for Yourself

I have not always cared for myself to the level that my mind, body and soul needs to thrive. Back in the day as a working single mother of two young girls, I would change "hats" from mom to cop to undercover prostitute in just one day! By the time I retired as a police officer, my adrenals were shot, and I was exhausted. That is why I now look at self-care as a necessity, not just a luxury. You must create a clear picture of the level of care you want for yourself, who you are at your core and remember to celebrate every step along the way.

I love the concept of managing your boundaries instead of your minutes. Being clear on what's important to you, knowing what you value and safeguarding what it takes to be that. The acronym C.A.R.E. is a daily reminder to me to be awake to the good stuff! "C" is for Cuisine—choosing quality organic delicious foods gives your mind, body, and soul the jet fuel it needs. "A" is for Awareness—giving yourself the gift of silence in nature or in journaling to feel your grace and power leading you on your path. "R" is for Rest—I love the cultures that embrace the nap! The indulgence of an afternoon nap or waking up in the morning fully rested sets the stage to be ready for anything. "E" is for Exercise—We are physical beings. Movement is the true medicine your body needs.

The more you have consistent morning and evening routines for your self-care, the better everything else runs in your day. What do you need to be at your best?

Life: Living In Freedom Epically!

Living your SPAlife is a lifestyle, a feeling, a mindset. It's also the miracles you may not notice in day-to-day life.

Nothing gives you a better perspective than getting out of your regular surroundings. A chance to know and grow - know thyself more deeply and grow into the next best version of yourself. The foundation to freedom for me is Faith ~Family ~ Friends ~ Food ~ Focus.

Remember L.I.F.E. is to live. You are either Living or longing. Be IN each and every moment. Embrace the Freedom to express how you want to live. And don't miss an opportunity to soar and see how epically and extraordinary everything really is!

Learn more at: www.dianehalfman.com

DIANE HALFMAN

It was never Diane Halfman's plan to walk the streets and become a prostitute, let alone get involved with vicious gangs and narcotics. Danger became a way of life for Diane, forcing her to carry a gun in her hand every day for 10 years. You see, Diane Halfman was an undercover cop for the San Diego Police Department. Her job was to infiltrate the gangs and prostitutes, bust the John's, bring 'em down, and clean up the streets.

Medically retired from the police department as a result of a training accident, Diane took her experience along with her Master's in Human Resources Management and Certification as an Ultimate Game of Life Coach to pioneer the creation of her own company, SPAlife. SPA is an acronym for Seek Power Always. Her podcast, "Live Your SPAlife," is a call to action for all women to define and create the life they truly want.

As a productivity consultant, Diane Halfman travels the country speaking, consulting, and conducting workshops and seminars dedicated to helping overwhelmed women entrepreneurs and corporate leaders move from a life of emergency to emergence. Diane possesses a unique set of skills and life experiences that allow her to coach, guide, and demonstrate the very techniques she used to RESET her own life and those of countless others. Her passion is to teach women how to be their own COP—walking in the world with more Confidence, Optimism, and Power.

S.P.A.R.K.

Significance • Pursue • Ascend • Reach • Kinetic

JEN DU PLESSIS

How many times have you been told – by yourself or someone else – that you "can't"? *Can't* could mean anything from your personal to professional life, but it isn't the specifics that matter. What does matter? Learning to tell yourself that you *can*.

What do you need to propel yourself from *can't* to *can*? What steps do you need to take that will lead you to confidently say "Go ahead, tell me I can't!"?

Lighting that fire—or any fire for that matter—begins with one thing: S.P.A.R.K. Just Five simple words to help you on your journey to "*can:*" Significance, Pursue, Ascend, Reach, and Kinetic.

Overcoming nearly any challenge begins with understanding Significance. Importance is a key part of the definition of significance – knowing and truly believing that you are important, and worthy, is crucial. Most of us are in touch with our dreams and desires, on some level at least. The challenge is getting started on the path from dream to reality. Assigning significance to our goals leads to exploring our lives deeply and bringing about ultimate possibilities.

The word significance has its roots in several words meaning "energy or force." When we open ourselves up to self-evaluation, we discover and reveal our true gifts, our true powers. Most important, we learn the significance of failures that lurk in our past. This self-realization and belief in ourselves and our abilities is what gives us power. Remember, even our failures are significant. Not only do we learn from them, the lessons they provide can only make a contingency plan even better.

Establishing goals and understanding significance is merely the first step. Those goals, or dreams, can never become reality if we don't Pursue them. Many times, what prevents us from taking this step is fear—fear of the unknown, fear of failure, and fear of taking a risk.

Pursuit of any goal will always involve some degree of risk. But so does *not* pursuing your dreams – in fact, that can often be even riskier. Calculate the risk, plan accordingly, and put your plan into motion.

Be realistic when you write your plan for success. Don't give yourself more than you can handle at any given time. Start by figuring out the most important step you need to take first and begin from there. And keep moving up – in other words, Ascend. Do something each day, no matter how small, that moves you closer to your goal.

Think of your ascension toward your goal as an evolutionary process. It won't occur overnight, and it will require many different steps, and setbacks, along the way. You will certainly be faced with letting go of old habits which may be holding you back. You might consider abandoning beliefs you've held true for decades. You could even find yourself adjusting your entire mindset completely.

Those ideas may sound a bit scary, which is what stifles so many people from making the leap from "plan" to "action." It's easy to forget that we aren't alone in our journey—no matter what our final destination may be. That's why it's so important to develop a solid support system. To do that, you must Reach out.

Asking others for help or guidance can be daunting. Some people don't want to be a burden; for others, it's a sense of pride and fear of appearing weak. The irony is that it's none of those things—in fact, it's usually the complete opposite.

Reaching your goals requires reaching out to stay focused on the bigger picture. Listening and talking to others provides a different perspective and can help retain, or maintain, focus. By doing so, you gradually build a support system you can tap into when you're venturing off course or you've come upon an obstacle you're not sure how to manage. Even the most seemingly solid plans will have glitches—it's how you handle them that matters and what keeps you moving forward.

In physics, the energy an object has due to its motion is known as kinetic energy. The journey to success is exactly that—energy in motion that can also be turned into power. *Our* energy being converted to *our* power to accomplish and achieve. Our personal energy comes from understanding our purpose, as well as our ability to positively contribute and build our legacy.

Coincidentally, one synonym for kinetic is "sparky." Think of your voyage to success as a lively, or sparky, one. It won't be boring; you'll meet new people along the way; you will definitely fall down and get back up; and, most important, you will emerge a profoundly happier individual. But none of this is possible without the energy needed to keep moving forward toward your goal.

Confidence in yourself means a realistic sense of, and secure knowledge in, your capabilities. Trust in yourself; acceptance of yourself, as well as knowing your strengths and weaknesses, will give you a sense of control in your life, which will, in turn, help you along the path to achieving your dreams and goals. It will give you the S.P.A.R.K you need to look your goals right in the eyes and say, "Go ahead, tell me I can't; I will show you I *can!*"

Learn more at: https://linktr.ee/jenduplessis

JEN DU PLESSIS

Jen is America's Lifestyle Business Master who helps sales professionals who feel overwhelmed and stressed out because of business trying to multiply results in record time, to have the courage to say yes to their personal lives.

In her career in the financial services industry, Jen was listed in the Top 200 of nationally-ranked mortgage originators and funded over $1 Billion in mortgage loans during her 37-year tenure.

She is recognized as an Influencer in her industry as a best-selling author, top podcast host, and charismatic speaker, sharing stages with such icons as Darren Hardy, Tony Robbins, Les Brown, James Dentley, Jeff Hoffman, Alec Stern, and Barbara Corcoran.

Jen believes that entrepreneurs can Live their Legacy while Building it!

S.W.I.T.C.H.

4 S's • Window and the Mirror • I Trio • Take the Time it Takes • Check Before You Correct • 3 Power HOW's of Leadership

BEN WARD

How to Make the S.W.I.T.C.H. from Selling to Leading

One question I get asked a lot is, "What's the secret to transitioning successfully into leadership? What does it take to go from being great at sales, to becoming great at leading other people?" It's one thing to know how to succeed yourself, it's another thing to know how to help others succeed.

In this chapter, I share the number one key I've found working with tens of thousands of sales leaders over the last 20 years, on what it takes to successfully transition into leadership, duplicate yourself, and get leveraged results with your team.

This key is embedded into an acronym, "S.W.I.T.C.H."

"S" - The 4 S's

#1 = Self

When you're on your own, it's all about you, but living by the seven most important words as a leader will steer you in the right direction to gain the respect and trust of the people you lead. *"It's not about you, it's about them."*

#2 = Selfless

Remember the golden rule? Do unto others as you would have done unto you.

This is good advice, but there is a rule that trumps this, the Platinum Rule: Do unto others as **they** would have done unto **them**. To apply this successfully, start with getting to know the people you lead. Find meaningful ways to serve them in ways they like to be served—not just ways that YOU like to be served.

#3 = Seeing

A super-power in leadership is the ability to see people as if they are what they could and ought to be. I love this quote from the ancient philosopher Goethe, "If you treat a man as he is, he will stay as he is. But if you treat him as if he were what he could and ought to be, he will become what he could and ought to become." This hits at the heart of leadership and influence, because giving people a name and reputation to live up to, is a powerful way to inspire others to want to rise up to that belief.

#4 = Serving

We can serve people in two ways: with a heart at peace, or with a heart at war. Let me illustrate. Recently, I did the dishes and when I started out, I was just trying to be helpful. Midway through, when scrubbing some caked-on oatmeal off one of the dishes, I began to shift my focus into blaming my wife for not rinsing them earlier (it would have been so easy!). Then I started thinking of how amazing I am for being here doing the dishes after a long day away from home, justifying my blaming heart. By the end of my dish session, I was ticked off cleaning those dishes. Here's the thing, the dishes got done. But they got done in two very different ways. First with a "heart at peace," just trying to be helpful, and then mid-way through, I was scrubbing them with a "heart at war!" The challenge is to serve more often with a heart at peace—when you do, watch as your leadership influence skyrockets.

"W" – The Window and the Mirror

When things go right, look out a window on who you can recognize. When things go wrong, look at a mirror to take responsibility. Where you choose to put your focus can make all the difference in your ability to influence the people you lead. One question to ask yourself is, after the victory, who holds the trophy? It can be challenging to give the trophy away to someone else. A lot of leaders struggle here. I invite you to **loosen your grip on the trophy and watch as your leadership influence skyrockets!**

"I" - The "I Trio"

We tend to hold onto this one without even realizing it. I'll never forget when one of my mentors pulled me aside after a training I gave with my team. She asked me how it went from my perspective? I told her I thought it went great but asked what she thought. She said, "Your message was good, but you talked about yourself the entire time. I lost count of the Me's, Myself's and I's, after about twenty of them in the first five minutes." I was stunned! This was not what I was expecting. I had no idea and hadn't remembered saying even one of them.

If you continue to make it about yourself, you will be missing the mark on what it takes to successfully influence others at the highest level. Remember, it's not about you, it's about them.

Try it for 24 hours! Find an accountability partner and tell them, "If you hear me say the words me, myself, or I, anytime in the next 24 hours, I give you permission to _____." (hit me in the arm, give me a cross-eyed look, have me pay you $5 dollars each time). You decide, but set the stakes high enough so you don't want to pay that price. Put this into play today and watch your leadership influence skyrocket!

"T" - Take the TIME It Takes

One day, an incredible mentor, "Papa Hyde," said, "If you take the time it takes, it takes less time." This was super profound, because as a leader, oftentimes we have to slow down and take the necessary time to really understand what's going on with the people we are leading. It's a natural tendency, especially for new leaders to jump straight into teaching mode, or challenging or even correcting, without taking the time that it takes to align with and meet a person where they're at to effectively lead them. "Before I say follow me, I find you." – John Maxwell. When you take the time it takes, it takes less time — and watch your leadership influence skyrocket!

"C" - Correction

One of the biggest mistakes I see new leaders make is jumping straight into correction with the people they lead. This is like pulling the pin in a grenade and throwing the grenade at your own feet, blowing up your ability to successfully influence the people you lead. Often, resentment is the result of poorly executed correction, and relationships suffer — you know what I'm talking about! I would highly advise not going straight into correction mode, but FIRST DO THIS:

"3 Checks Before You Correct"

First, check your intent. Is the correction motivated by a sincere desire to be helpful to them? Dig deep on this one to make sure your intent is in the right place, and not motivated out of a selfish desire to gratify your pride. Second, check their "vital few." The vital few are three key areas that are important to check in order to properly diagnose how we can help the people we lead. The three questions put very simply are ... **Where's their mind at? Where's their heart at? What are their feet doing?**

To gauge their **mind**, these example questions are so simple that some people might dismiss them: How's it going today? Or, what's been on your mind lately? Or even, how are you showing up today? Then you listen carefully. You can learn a lot about where their mind is in this way.

For their **heart**, ask them what makes them tick. What gets them out of bed in the morning? What are they passionate about? What do they dream about? My mentor, Brian Tracy, would ask me, "Ben, what one thing would you dare to dream if you knew you could not fail?" I loved that question, because it drove me to dig deep and revealed what my heart longed for.

Their **feet** refer to their actions and results. To find out why they are getting those results, look closer at how they are spending their time. What does their calendar look like? What do their numbers look like? The mind and heart control the feet. So if the feet aren't moving, or they are headed in the wrong direction, it's almost always an opportunity with their mind or their heart.

The third and final check before correcting is to check the expectations you have set. Make sure you have set very clear expectations and that they are aware of them in advance. If they are not clear, take a step back and don't launch into correction. Instead, teach them!

When you pause and check these three areas before launching into correction mode (intent, vital few, and expectations), watch as your leadership influence skyrockets!

"H" - The "3 Power How's of Leadership"

Asking and answering these three questions will provide a huge advantage for you as a leader. Ask these questions deeply, honestly, and moment by moment in your work. Success will grow naturally out of the honest questions you are willing to ask yourself and answer transparently.

*How am I a problem for others?
*How can I be more helpful to everyone?
*How can I be a better leader for my team?

As these questions dominate your thinking, you will find yourself focused more and more on how you can help the people you lead achieve results. Write these questions out everywhere. Memorize them. Write them on flashcards and stick them in your pocket. Create these questions as an alert in your phone—one question at a time going off at different times during the day. Get extreme—write them on your bathroom mirror! But make a commitment to etch these three questions into your mind! The deeper you go to answer them, the more likely you are to gain the respect of the people you lead.

When you honestly ask yourself these questions and take action to apply the answer, watch as your leadership influence skyrockets!

Making the transition into leadership can be challenging, but I'm confident as you S.W.I.T.C.H your mindset and implement these principles you can and will be successful!

Here's a cheat sheet to remember **how to make the S.W.I.T.C.H. from selling to leading.**

Learn more at www.benward.com

BEN WARD

 Ben Ward is a sales and leadership master with over 20 years' experience in executive leadership training and development. A sought-after keynote speaker, mentor, and strategic advisor, he founded Forward Leadership as a result of his personal obsession for continuous improvement and passion for helping others grow and develop.

\

T.H.I.N.

Tribe • Health • Intuition • Network

KAROLINA HOBSON

Thin, Rich, and Happy

Happiness comes to us in stages, which are not always in a predictable pattern or order, and typically involves much more than our state of mind or uplifted mood; it involves living a rich life. Naturally, happiness is about achieving a certain level of well-being and well-living and invariably has a significant impact on how we navigate our paths to success and accomplishment. In turn, living a rich life does not always entail amassing a large amount of money. Rather, a truly rich, wealthy life means living to the best of our abilities and remaining in touch with our individual purpose.

Unfortunately, accomplishing such a life experience is not always easy and necessitates that we focus on key elements and efforts in order to elevate our mindset. T.H.I.N. does not, of course, refer to physical stature but rather to four primary components of success and happiness: Tribe, Health, Intuition, and Network.

We all belong to a tribe, which may manifest differently for each person, but tends to consist of those closest to us, typically friends and family. No one is able to flourish on his or her own. Rather, we rely more often than we realize on friends and family for support. Not only does this reliance enhance our mental well-being in difficult times, but it satisfies an innate need to feel a sense of belonging to something more than just ourselves.

Each person in our tribe serves a different purpose in our lives. When we need to talk or vent, some may be good listeners. When we feel down or stressed, others may have a knack for cheering us up. Such diversity in a tribe aids in decision-making and problem-solving, and the support we receive can and does help reduce stress and provide a healthful outlet.

Clearly, minimizing stress in our lives has a tremendous impact on our health, both physically and spiritually. By protecting our minds and bodies from the actual physiological symptoms of stress, we can strive to improve our physical health. In turn, by increasing our sense of purpose and meaning, we can enhance our spiritual health.

The benefits of achieving and maintaining physical health may be more evident than the concept of spiritual health, but all health issues, whether a broken bone or a broken psyche, require a form of healing. Spiritual health helps guide us toward a significant purpose and provides a sense of selflessness. Perhaps most important is the way in which spiritual health helps us to find hope in difficult times, provides us with systems of principles and morals, enables us to live lives according to those systems, and directs us toward meaning in our everyday lives.

Being in touch with our spiritual self is similar to, although somewhat different from, being in touch with our inner self, also known as our intuition. We have all experienced, from time to time, an unconscious feeling that motivates us to act. That feeling is intuition: our unconscious ability to know or feel something in the absence of conscious reasoning. Although we often fail to rely upon it, we are all equipped with intuition.

Just as we cannot choose to possess or impose upon intuition, strong emotions beyond our control can cause our instinctive reactions to become blurred. Such emotions can often have an impact on how we feel when we are upset. The "out of sorts" feeling that typically accompanies a sense of distress may very well be due to a detachment from our inner self.

Furthermore, research has linked strong intuition to successful individuals. Tapping into our ability to "listen to our gut" can have a significant impact on our personal and professional lives. Using intuition to read people, by paying attention to the "energy" they project, makes for better leaders in business settings. Indeed, listening to what our instinct is telling us can help mitigate and resolve awkward or perplexing social situations.

Our intuition is also useful when we think about creating and growing a network. Our network is different from our tribe in that a tribe supports our personal life while a network provides support professionally and externally. Growing a network means finding other groups or individuals who share our interests or goals. These relationships are a key part of our journey to success.

Our networks are certainly not just there to give *us* something; it is important that we are willing to reciprocate. A good approach to growing our networks is always to consider giving more than we receive. In that way, a network can become a wonderful way for us to come up with new ideas, learn new things, and gain new perspectives. Sharing information within our networks is an essential key to successful decision-making and problem-resolution as it provides insight that we may not have stumbled upon on our own. Whenever ideas come from those whom we look up to or trust, we gain, with a fresh perspective, a vision that helps us navigate the road to success and overcome inevitable barriers.

Clearly, within a vacuum, we can never realize a life lived T.H.I.N., rich, and happy. A truly fulfilled life composed of achievement and success, friends and loved ones, and spiritual and physical health is founded in our concerted efforts to know our capabilities and, in turn, use them to the best of our ability. Fortunately, wealth that is beyond the mere monetary or material kind is all around us, within our grasp. It is never too late to take that first step.

KAROLINA HOBSON

Karolina Hobson believes that in order to become T.H.I.N., RICH, and HAPPY, you must envision your dreams, trust the process, and invest in your personal development and growth.

Raised by an immigrant mother, who set her up for success by showing her everything IS possible, Karolina has learned and invested in her T.H.I.N., TRIBE, HEALTH, INTUITION, and NETWORK to find her rich and happy.

Karolina is a successful entrepreneur, contributor to publications such as *Forbes, Newsweek,* and *Fast Company,* an investor, and social-selling pro. She holds a Bachelor's Degree in Business Administration and Management from San Diego State University and has more than 15 years' experience in sales, social media, leadership, and business solutions within the media, marketing, sales, public relations, finance, and social organization industries.

She has a heart for serving others and pouring into her family, friends, and teams. She firmly believes in collaboration over competition, and she explains the importance of knowing and trusting your TRIBE, investing in HEALTH (mental, spiritual, and physical), using your INTUITION (trusting your gut), as well as developing your NETWORK (finding the right employers, groups, associations, and acquaintances). Karolina enjoys spending time with her husband and three kids at the beach or hiking. She is an avid concert go'er and loves working out.

T.I.N.T.

There • Is • No • They

JEFF HOFFMAN

Every day, all around us, we see problems. On TV, on the Internet, in social media, out our car window, everywhere. It might be a homeless person we drive by. It might be a news story about victims of crime. It might be children in another country who don't have food and don't even know where their next meal is coming from.

And what do we say when we see these things? I can tell you exactly what we say, because I have said it myself, too many times. We are all guilty of it. We say, "They should help those people." "They should do something." "They should feed those children." But if everyone looking at the problem says, "They should do something," then who is actually doing anything? That's right, no one.

TINT – There is No They

These are the four words that changed my life. The words that I point to when my friends ask me why I don't just retire and play golf. Because the world isn't going to get any better all by itself. Problems don't get solved by talking about them. Children don't eat just because we feel bad for them.

There is no they, because it's YOU.

Next time you see a real problem in the world, stand up and step out. Take ownership. Be accountable. Make a plan, and then GO DO SOMETHING. You don't need to know all the answers. You just have to START. Sometimes people see the size of the world's problems, and it makes them feel small and helpless. So they do nothing because they don't think they can do enough. But they're wrong.

Mother Teresa once said, "If you can't feed a hundred people, feed one." She was so right. "They" aren't coming to help. But you are, and you're already here. So look around your community, your neighborhood, the town you live in. Find someone who isn't as fortunate as you. And make the decision to help, to change someone's life by being in it. All you have to do is start.

To learn more, visit:

www.jeffhoffman.com and www.worldyourthhorizons.com

JEFF HOFFMAN

 Jeff Hoffman, an accomplished entrepreneur and innovator in the fields of Internet, e-commerce, and entertainment, is Executive in Residence and Founding Director of UA's Center for Experiential Learning, Entrepreneurship and Civic Engagement. The new center will significantly expand opportunities for students across campus to experience service learning, co-ops, internships, and other opportunities for civic and entrepreneurial engagement. The center will connect students with industry leaders and alumni mentors.

He is a founder/partner in ColorJar, a venture accelerator firm that helps entrepreneurs and small business owners launch and grow new business ventures. In this capacity, Jeff works as a virtual CEO with startup companies worldwide. He previously served as the CEO of Enable Holdings, Inc., an international leader among excess inventory solutions companies. Enable Holdings, a publicly traded company, operates online sites uBid.com and RedTag.com. and has sold more than $2 billion worth of consumer goods since its launch.

Hoffman is perhaps best known as a founder and CEO in the Priceline.com family of companies, where Jeff led the development and launch of Priceline's consumer company (Priceline YardSale). Hoffman also served as an executive in Walker Digital, the parent company of Priceline and one of the country's most innovative creators of intellectual property and new business models.

Hoffman received a Lifetime Achievement Award in Entrepreneurship from the National CEO Council in 2010, and the 2012 Champion of Entrepreneurship Award from JP Morgan Chase, Citibank, and Rising Tide Capital. He was inducted into the Hall of Fame for Entrepreneurs by the

International Association of College Entrepreneurs in 2010. Hoffman is an accomplished professional and motivational speaker and has been a featured business expert on Fox News, Fox Business, CNN, CNN International, Bloomberg News, CNBC, ABC, and NPR, and in publications, including *Forbes, Inc., Time, Fast Company*, and the *Wall Street Journal.*

T.O.M.A.

Top • Of • Mind • Attention

CHARLIE CINA

Intention is a powerful word that is very connected and in alignment with the word "commitment." If you're going to make a commitment, you better have the right intentions to back it up and see it through to fruition. The definition of intention is a mental state that represents a commitment to carry out an action or actions in the future. Intention involves mental activities such as planning, forethought, and aiming for a target or result.

Wayne Dyer said, "Our intention creates our reality." When I wake up in the morning, it is my intention to expose and close. I must expose my products and services to as many people as I can daily. I must expose the solutions that my products and services can offer to a particular company or individual.

No matter what product or service you provide, it will most likely solve a problem that falls into one of these buckets. Your solution will help people make money, save money, improve their health, improve their financial status, or better their lifestyle. So, here is my intention—my intention is to get your ATTENTION. When I get your attention, I want you to pay attention. When you pay attention, eventually you will pay me for my attention. So, your intention should be to get attention.

When you get attention, get people to pay attention, then—eventually—they will pay you for your attention. This isn't a rap or nursery rhyme. Here in reality, words are things. Words trigger pictures, which trigger emotions, that gets people to take action.

Words are written code, verbal code, and words are connected. There are word formulas and sequences that when executed and delivered properly, will help you take quantum leaps. The right words will help you stay Top of Mind with people that matter, and the end result will be profitable relationships, revenue streams, and a level of success you desire.

Now, in order to create Top of Mind Awareness, you must create multiple points of contact. Staying top of mind will require thanking people, showing people that you remember them, celebrating them, and having the authentic intention of building a relationship. Strong and powerful relationships are paramount in life and in business. To stay Top of Mind, I personally make it my mission to send people personal notes, birthday cards, thank you cards, send flowers, and I've even been known to send a pizza.

It's really simple … people like to be recognized, people like to feel significant, and everybody appreciates an authentic friendship, whether it's personal or business. Many people say business is not personal, but nothing could be further from the truth. Business is definitely personal. It's my profession, it's what I do, it's the product and service I represent. It's how I feed my family. It's the value that I provide to the free market.

So, business is definitely personal, and I make it my job and my duty to make sure that my clients become my friends. Now, some people may disagree with that, however, I'm here to tell you that it has worked for me. Most business relationships I build result in friendships and ultimately result in long-term revenue relationships. These long-term revenue relationships also produce abundant referrals that are ultimately qualified prospects and dream clients. So, here are some great tools and moves that I use to stay top of mind and let my friends and clients know they're appreciated.

After you've met with a client for a personal meeting, lunch, or dinner, send a personal note recapping briefly what was discussed and let them know how much you appreciate the relationship. Send a card for a birthday, wedding anniversary, business anniversary, or whatever celebratory event that may be going on in that person's life at that particular time. I use a service that allows me to custom make cards by incorporating photos of the person I'm sending the card to. The service also allows me to send candy, brownies, cookies, and other various gifts with the card.

I used this service to send a thank you to one of my good friends and client, Anthony Delmedico. Anthony is the founder of Storm Ventures Group, and he hosts a yearly conference called Win the Storm for over 2,000 roofing contractors. Last year, he invited me to speak at his conference and deliver my Expose and Close marketing message. After the event, I sent him a personalized card and brownies. Now, Anthony is a very successful businessman, and he has the money and wherewithal to buy anything he chooses. However, when a man of his caliber picks up the phone to express how genuinely appreciative he was to receive a thank you card with a box of brownies, you really start to realize that it's the simple things that people truly appreciate.

I have also utilized this service as a marketing strategy to get people's attention. I have a list of the top people I want to prospect. Sometimes emails, video emails, texts, knocks, and show ups just don't work. In these cases, I'll send a card. I will custom make a card with a picture that complements that individual and their business. I'll put their company logo on the card, as well.

Again, the objective is to get people's attention and one of the main ways is to show them a picture of themselves. So, when they open the box, there is a card in it with their picture on the front. Inside the card is a Starbucks gift card and a message that says, "I have been trying to connect with you for a cup of coffee. The coffee is on me, just let me know when you can carve out 15 minutes for a call. Look forward to speaking soon, Charlie."

Although nothing works 100 percent of the time, this potential million-dollar move gets me pretty darn close. I can get somebody's attention and schedule a 15 to 20-minute uninterrupted call and share with them who I am, what I do, and what problems I can help them solve. Now I have their full attention to educate them on how I can solve their problems, help them reach their goals, and generate more revenue.

To learn more visit, me at charliecina.com and exposeandclose.com

CHARLIE CINA

Charlie Cina captivates his audiences and teaches them how to master the right mindset, missions, and moves to reach their personal potential to drive massive revenue. Through his writings, speaking, and consulting, he has built a vast group of followers known as Disciples of Sales. Charlie believes that the ability to present and persuade are necessary life skills that everyone needs to succeed. He will teach you that your primary responsibility in business is to expose your brand, expose your products, expose your services, and expose your solutions to build long-lasting revenue relationships. Charlie has leveraged his expertise in sales and marketing to work with billion-dollar brands like Pepsi, Mandarin Oriental Hotels, and The Wynn Resort. He has acquired as clients the top motivational speakers and trainers in the world like Tony Robbins, Les Brown, and Eric Thomas. His 30 years of boots on the ground and under-fire sales experience has led him to create the proven techniques and strategies to activate, acquire, and achieve massive success. Charlie will transfer to you his simple formula to make sales easy, so anyone who implements it can potentially connect with high-level clients and billion-dollar companies.

T.T.E.

Talk • To • Everyone

DR. GREG REID

We are surrounded by stories. Some are boisterous and bright; and some are tucked away silently in the most unlikely vessels. There are so many stories to tell and be told, yet far too many are not. They remain hidden and protected, often waiting for someone to drag them out into the light.

These stories belong to all of us, and there's only one way to expose them — TTE. Talk To EVERYONE. Many people naturally command attention, which makes it easy to forget that there are other people in the room. The most wonderful stories, the most eye-opening wisdom, and the most life-altering lessons can be found at the most unexpected times in the most unlikely storyteller.

If you've spent any amount of time in an airport bookshop, it should be no surprise that the vast majority of biographies and autobiographies belong to celebrities, CEOs, or other widely known people. Their names alone are the marketing plan, but that also leaves most with the instinctive, yet erroneous, notion that only the successful or wealthy have stories worth sharing or hearing.

Consider how many people we encounter daily—whether at the supermarket, the gym, or the coffee shop—do we ever stop to think what stories the strangers we pass may have to tell? Typically, we avert our eyes, pretend to be extremely busy on our phones or engrossed in a book we are barely reading. All of this to avoid making eye contact, let alone starting an actual conversation.

Instead, we need to think of these casual strangers as special ties to the outside world who, by stopping to talk to them, could fill us with inspiration, new experiences, and knowledge. These people are as vital to our growth as family and close friends. Stop for a moment and count how many times a day you've avoided even so much as a "hello" in passing. Each of those moments was a missed opportunity to potentially enrich your day, and life, through a conversation with someone unfamiliar and new.

Technology has hindered our ability—and in some cases, desire—to actually *talk* to people. A world of communication that is centered on acronym-filled texting or shorthand emails has taken a toll on how, and how often, we communicate. Behind the shadow of a computer monitor or phone screen, it's much more difficult to reach out to strangers. Out in the "real world," it's possible to create environments in which we *can* talk to complete strangers and venture outside of our comfort zones. Remembering that there is much more out there than our tight-knit circle of familiarity can be the key to broadening our horizons and expanding our perception of so many aspects of life.

Tiptoeing away from the safety of our social bubble is a major roadblock for many of us. Approaching someone we don't know can be daunting – there's no way to know how they will respond or if they will even be receptive. Unknowns are never comfortable. Ideas and beliefs are held dear to our hearts, and by avoiding strangers, we avoid either of those being challenged. What if they caused us to look at an idea or belief differently? What if they help us to realize that a truth we've clung to for a lifetime is, in fact, wrong?

The problem is, while the answers to those questions can be uncomfortable, we actually do ourselves more harm by only talking to or socializing with those who mirror our ideas, beliefs, and even stories. The tendency to do so is most likely born from what we all heard growing up: *"Don't talk to strangers."* While this is certainly sage advice for a child, when applied to our adult lives, the opposite is true. It implies that we should surround ourselves with those who are just like us and discourage us from making the trip out of our comfort zones to meet new people. Even our closest friends were strangers at one point.

Everyone needs knowledge and experience that extends beyond what limited daily interactions can teach. We need to talk to EVERYONE to improve our understanding of people, from a cultural perspective, as well. Improving our understanding of various societal groups can never be a bad thing. Ultimately, our sense of self will improve, along with our perspective on all aspects of life.

Critical listening skills will be sharpened also. Engaging with someone in conversation that consists of a barrage of questions surely to result in "yes or no" answers has little value. The true benefit of talking to everyone is to expand knowledge and perception as far as it will go. Asking thoughtful, engaging, and genuine questions is exactly how to get there. Listening is the key to get your mind thinking about ways to add value, while also truly hearing what someone is saying.

The next time you're at the gym, the café, the post office, or even riding the bus, turn to a stranger and say "hello." If you're lucky, you will get to listen to their story.

Learn more at: https://gregreid.com

DR. GREG REID

For over 25 years, Greg has inspired millions of people to take personal responsibility to step into the potential of their greatness and, as such, his life of contribution has been recognized by government leaders, a foreign princess, as well as luminaries in education, business, and industry.

Mr. Reid has been published in over 115 books, including 32 best-sellers in 45 languages. Titles such as *Stickability: The Power of Perseverance; The Millionaire Mentor,* and *Three Feet from Gold: Turn Your Obstacles into Opportunities,* have inspired countless readers to understand that the most valuable lessons we learn are also the easiest ones to apply.

Greg Reid is known best for being Founder of Secret Knock, a *Forbes, Enterpreneur,* and *Inc.* magazine top-rated event focused on partnership, networking, and business development. He is the producer of the Oscar-qualified film, *Wish Man,* based on the creator of the Make A Wish Foundation, streaming on Netflix now.

For his work in mentoring youth in his hometown of San Diego, Mr. Reid was honored by the White House, where a former President commended Greg for his work for positively working with youth through a local mentorship program. And if that is not enough, recently Greg was honored with a star of the infamous Las Vegas Walk of Stars.

Made in the USA
Las Vegas, NV
13 July 2021

26407577R00115